Praise for *Arrangeme*

"[Amy] Key's background as a poet gorgeously lyrical, but she is alsc colder, harsher parts of being single. *Arrangements in Blue* is a short read, but each page feels so full and worth savouring. I already have friends who have sent me screenshots of the parts that made them feel so seen. And I have sent them mine."
—Hollie Richardson, *Guardian*

"Amy Key writes with such tenderness and insight about a life without romantic love at its center, exacting as to its impoverishments, exultant over its many and unexpected riches."
—Olivia Laing, author of *The Lonely City*

"From grief to anger to full-throttled joy, Amy Key hits every note of feeling with perfect pitch. . . . An absolutely gorgeous work."
—Heather Christle, author of *The Crying Book*

"Filled with lyrical turns of phrase, this insightful take on living solo will appeal to poets, dreamers, and anyone marching to the beat of their own drum. It's a lush and moving memoir."
—*Publishers Weekly*, starred review

"There is a whole life pulsing within these pages, written with both clarity and eloquence, a glittering brightness that glints like stars in a navy velvet sky. A book to be read in astonishment and in admiration. Bewitching."
—Doireann Ní Ghríofa, author of *A Ghost in the Throat*

"Courageous. . . . [A] bracingly honest read."
—Alexis Burling, *San Francisco Chronicle*

"Amy Key's extraordinary *Arrangements in Blue* isn't merely a commentary on Joni Mitchell's *Blue*, but something bolder, more personal and shape-shafting, in line with Joni's own art in that it takes no starting point for granted."
—Paul Lisicky, author of *Later: My Life at the Edge of the World*

"[*Arrangements in Blue*] asks how to build a good life when you don't have what you want—and how to do so without denying what it is that you want, or the possibility that what you want may come along."

—Hannah Rosefield, *New Republic*

"Illuminating, instructive, and unsettling, [Key's] book examines sexual attraction, unrequited love, strategies to numb rejection, and the possibilities of intimacy and fulfillment in a life lived in the absence of romantic love—even as she recognizes that 'if you ask yourself hard questions, you must be prepared not to find an answer.'"

—Glenn Altschuler, *Psychology Today*

"[Key's] nonfiction debut is a courageously honest meditation on her partnerless life, and her inward and outward search for all the things a soulmate was supposed to deliver."

—Emma John, *Guardian*

"There's nothing poor-me about *Arrangements in Blue*; in Key's hands, solitary life becomes more capacious—and more complicated—than I ever thought possible."

—Sophia M. Stewart, *Millions*

"Amy writes with rare integrity, courage, and style about the pursuit of love—it's somehow both consoling and provoking, and a beautiful and necessary book."

—Sarah Perry, author of *The Essex Serpent*

"Key's prose melds the investigative with the personal . . . *Arrangements in Blue* feels more akin to a Joni Mitchell song—strong as it is tentative, wavering as it is hard-hitting, an essay collection whose thoughts rise and fall like ocean waves with Key examining both the wreckage and the treasures that find their way to shore."

—Sadaf Ferdowsi, *NewCity*

Arrangements in Blue

Arrangements in Blue

Notes on Loving and Living Alone

AMY KEY

LIVERIGHT PUBLISHING CORPORATION
A DIVISION OF W. W. NORTON & COMPANY
Independent Publishers Since 1923

First American Edition 2023
First published as a Liveright paperback 2024
First published in the United Kingdom by Jonathan Cape in 2023.

For information about special discounts for bulk purchases, please contact W. W. Norton Special Sales at specialsales@wwnorton.com or 800-233-4830

Manufacturing by Lakeside Book Company
Production manager: Louise Mattarelliano

Library of Congress Cataloging-in-Publication Data

Names: Key, Amy, author.
Title: Arrangements in Blue : notes on loving and living alone / Amy Key.
Description: First American edition. | New York : Liveright, 2023.
Identifiers: LCCN 2023006585 | ISBN 9781324091738 (hardcover) | ISBN 9781324091745 (epub)
Subjects: LCSH: Key, Amy. | Women poets, English—Biography. | Single people—Great Britain—Social conditions—21st century. | Solitude. | Love. | Mitchell, Joni. Blue.
Classification: LCC PR6111.E788 Z46 2023 | DDC 821/.92—dc23/eng/20230405
LC record available at https://lccn.loc.gov/2023006585

ISBN 978-1-324-09516-3 pbk.

Liveright Publishing Corporation, 500 Fifth Avenue, New York, N.Y. 10110
www.wwnorton.com

W. W. Norton & Company Ltd., 15 Carlisle Street, London W1D 3BS

1 2 3 4 5 6 7 8 9 0

This book is for anyone who needs
a love story of being alone

I felt the world all around me . . . That's how that whole *Blue* chapter ends, and it's also where the next one begins.

JONI MITCHELL

It's love I want, and the song which follows love.

RODDY LUMSDEN

Contents

LOVE

looking for something, what can it be

When I travelled, alone, to Los Angeles in early 2020, a taxi driver asked me why I'd come. I told him I was there to write about the singer-songwriter Joni Mitchell. It felt good to have a story.

'Joni Mitchell, Joni Mitchell,' he said. 'I'm just thinking if I know someone who knows Joni.'

I didn't say anything.

'Hmm, wait, I think I do. I've known the musician Gillian Welch for like twenty years,' he said, 'I'll give her a call. Maybe Gillian can hook you up, get you five minutes on the phone with her or something. Here, take my number.'

I took his number even though I knew I would not call him. I was attracted to the idea of being someone who would call him. And while I did hope to write about Joni, she wasn't why I was there. I'd had the trip planned long before that idea came along. I was there to write and think. But I didn't expect much of myself. My friend and poetry mentor Roddy had died the month before. I arrived with a grief that I hoped might melt into California's huge horizons. I hoped newness might knock grief clean out of me.

*

Joni Mitchell's album *Blue* has been part of my interior world for thirty years. My copy of it, on vinyl, has grown warped from being kept in direct sunlight, scratched from my careless ways with record sleeves and liners. When I play the record, it sounds as though it's being received from space – the music delivered through a fuzzy channel of feedback. It's been so well used as to take on the quality of being commonplace, where dings and scratches and fading are accepted because of its sense of belonging to me. But I don't need to play the album to listen to it. I can sing it from start to finish, with all the emotional and tonal shifts, and often do. I can summon every element of the music in my head. My paternal grandma, Eva, used to say to me, 'Amy, I hear music.' I loved this mysterious declaration. I now know what she meant. Using thought as my instrument, I regularly play *Blue* from start to finish without a pause.

The album came out in 1971, seven years before I was born. It was Joni's fourth, recorded in LA, after she'd taken a year's break from touring. *Blue*'s songs hold within them the potency of that time taken for reflection. Joni was already enjoying success – her album *Clouds* won a Grammy for 'Best Folk Performance' in 1970, and *Ladies of the Canyon*, the record that came out before *Blue*, had sold over half a million copies. But *Blue* eclipsed what had gone before. The album's charting of love, loss and longing became a landmark for millions worldwide, across all decades of life. It's the kind of album people play one another in the early stages of a relationship to help express big feelings. That people will frame the front cover of and put on their wall. That someone might pull a lyric from for a tattoo. An album that people inherit from others emotionally. Even before I first heard her music, I accepted as fact that Joni was an important musician, part of popular music's canon in the same way as Prince, the Beatles, Diana Ross, Kate Bush. I don't know how this sense came about, but I instinctively knew that I would one day spend time with her music. Decide if Joni was going to be canon to me.

I think back to 1992 and the first time I heard *Blue*. My best friend had recently begun to have periods, and one had just started. She was sleeping over on the pull-out bed that lived under my own. We called it 'the surfboard'. My red and purple lava lamp was on, the rest of the lights were off. We listened to the album on cassette, borrowed from my older sister Rebecca. An emotional inheritance.

The first song is 'All I Want'. Into the dark cocoon of our sleepover, Joni sang 'I am on a lonely road and I am travelling, travelling, travelling, travelling, looking for something, what can it be?' I remember having a strange feeling, an anxiety-adjacent excitement, a bodily sense that I too would experience something transformative, and soon. I joined Joni on the road she was travelling. I knew I would not sleep until the cassette had clicked onto the B-side and I had heard the last note of the last song.

In my memory of that night, the lava lamp was like the pain my friend was experiencing, the hot red pulse of it. Pain as a red energy, as hypnotic. Pain that moves as an octopus might in the deep seas of womanhood and romantic grief – thresholds I had yet to cross. I was fourteen and yearning to swim in both.

That night *Blue* ignited my desire and ambition for romantic love, my idea of how I would press my heart against the world. What appealed, I think, was the way it described the complexities of love. It was the first representation of love that seemed truthful: love as best and worst, joy and sorrow. I'd hurt someone. They would hurt me. Love meant staying and going, the bothness of it suddenly clear. And love did not need to mean convention, perhaps not marriage, perhaps not children. The music's harmonic cascades in all their sprawling highs and lows mapped the course I, and romantic love, would take. *Blue* seemed to give me a complete palette to paint myself into all life's possibilities. I took in the album's emotional range, and it became innate. I accepted *Blue* as part of the language I had to express myself.

In early crushes and relationships, I'd test my feelings against *Blue*'s sentiments, as though the album provided an ultimate scale of intensity that would reveal whether the love had substance. Was this a love so strong I couldn't numb it out of myself with wine? Did it have the endurance of the northern star? Could it keep away my blues? Would it anchor me where I stood, or let me sail away? Looking back now, I think I tricked myself into believing almost all of my romantic attachments measured up against *Blue*'s scale. I accepted love would bring me pain, so much so that joyful love became not an expectation, but an occasional gift. Love meant being prepared to bleed. I was ready to commit to it.

But while I have certainly bled for romantic love, I've largely found myself living without it. The last time I had a boyfriend I was twenty-two. I'm about to turn forty-four. In my early years of knowing *Blue* I thought I was at the beginning of romantic love's presence in my life. All beginnings incorporate the potential for an end, I just had no idea how rapidly I'd get there.

Sometimes I read my teenage diaries intent on finding a solution to my lovelessness, or clues, at least, about why things have turned out this way. What ideas and behaviours took hold then, and might they give me keys to understanding myself? I've been troubled to read how I would passively respond to the desire another person had for me, as though their attraction was something I was subject to rather than a mutual occurrence. It seemed I'd been gripped by the idea of love as exquisite pain rather than joy. And I would rather have chosen pain, deception, abuse even, than been alone. In one entry, I wrote 'even being used would be better than this' – 'this' being romance's absence. My diaries from that time reveal a young woman desperate for romantic attachment, page after page accounting for being noticed and not being noticed by objects of desire. There is little else – no intellectualising, it's all pangs of longing.

At the back of one diary from 1995/6, between the ages of sixteen and seventeen, there is a list of boys I kissed or had an involvement with, and how long it lasted. Tim, Gregg, Craig (two months), Dave, Brian (two weeks), Adam, Gary, Peter, Gary, Craig. Sometimes these boys were so close together it was like they were cigarettes I lit from the end of the one I was smoking. I thought that list would go on forever.

In 'All I Want' Joni sings, 'I hate you some, I hate you some, I love you some'. A manifesto of romantic ambivalence, of how the mind 'see-saws' when you love. She plays a stringed instrument I had always assumed to be a guitar but now know is an Appalachian dulcimer, which she used for the first time on *Blue*. The dulcimer flits cleanly between chords, but is tonally nervy – a musical agitation – and Joni's mezzo-soprano voice glides above it, making full use of its range. I don't think 'I hate you some, I hate you some, I love you some' is intended to prize a love that is both hot and cold, cruel and kind; but I do think it was easy for me to manipulate her message for my own ends. To justify what I thought, what I did and what I was subject to as the natural or indeed ideal romantic experience.

In my first experience of unrequited love, at seventeen, I wrote obsessively about how I felt. No detail too small. I'd met him at the Riverside club, in Newcastle. I went every Friday night. It was summertime and we were there for my sister's birthday. She'd made us piña coladas before we went out – I'd never had a cocktail before, and I was greedy for the glamour of it. I wore a hot pink satin miniskirt, low on my hips. It had a skinny belt. On the dance floor, he came over and said, 'I like your belt.' That was all it took.

After we kissed he asked for my number. He told me he would call me the following Tuesday, and I had no doubt that he would. He was *so* into me. I was *such a nice kisser*. I was *so gorgeous*. There was some thrilling warm weather that week. Monday was spent wildly anticipating Tuesday. Tuesday came and went, hungry and insomniac. On the Wednesday I bargained with myself about why he'd not yet called. The pre-internet comfort of *he's lost my number*. I had a half-day at college, so went home, got an extension cord so I could bring a radio outside, opened all the windows so that I would hear the phone, and sat in the yard. I hoped I might get a tan in the narrow portion of sun that fanned across the yard during the afternoon. On the radio, they were leading with the story of Hugh Grant's arrest in

LA for paying a sex worker, Divine Brown, for a blow job. I felt I was getting purchase on this world of adults, where I drank cocktails, sunbathed, understood the subtext of 'a lewd act' and waited for boys to call me on the telephone. I spent the afternoon walking in and out of the house, checking the phone was definitely on the hook, calling 1571 to see if I'd missed a call. There were no calls. I was exquisitely agitated. There was the pain of rejection, but alongside that pain, there was the pleasure of desire. My body activated in an entirely new way, a way that called back to how it felt to first hear *Blue*. I'd turned seventeen that month. I felt that I was entering the world Joni had prepared me for. I wanted to feel girlhood exiting my body. The way I expected that to happen was through romantic love entering my body and conquering it.

I saw him at the nightclub again and again. One time in between kissing he asked me if I was seeing anyone else, and I said, 'No, I just want you.' Later that night he said to me 'I've been worried, about things you said. You don't want anyone else but me.' I tried to poke holes in what I'd said to him. To make it minuscule. Eventually he relaxed and asked me to come home with him. It was the first time I would deny what I wanted in the hope it might make me more desirable. That night I was desperate to lose my virginity. He tried for hours to press into me – dry despite my longing – while 'Wonderwall' by Oasis played on repeat, the cassette auto-turning from the A- to the B-side and back again. The next day I got the metro back from Newcastle to South Shields, my eyeliner from the night before still immaculate. Before reaching my house I called my friend Rachel on a payphone, asking her to say I'd stayed at hers if my parents asked. A couple of weeks later, when I'd not heard from him again, I wrote in my diary 'I love you. I love you. I hate myself and I hate you.' I hadn't realised, until now, that I was paraphrasing

Joni. After him, more short relationships followed this pattern. Then I got a serious boyfriend, which lasted a year; then another, almost a year. Another, and then nothing.

*

In a 2007 interview with the *Toronto Globe and Mail*, Joni was asked about how she tuned her guitar, an idiosyncratic tuning. She spoke of creating 'chords of inquiry', she wanted a sound like 'a question' in every chord. She even starts *Blue* with a question. *Looking for something, what can it be?* I think that's what arose for me in LA, a curiosity about how Joni saw the world, saw love, and the ways in which she had shaped me. So that is where I'll begin my own inquiry, into romantic love and its absence. I'll start with a *Blue* perspective, a filter to think through my own questions.

Blue has been a companion for thirty years now, and in it I keep finding something I need. First it was an impression of womanhood and romantic love that I could pursue. It then became a way to measure the gap between those dreams and my reality. But now it has given me an endeavour, one I've only just summoned the courage to begin. The more I have listened to the album, the more all the things I thought went hand in hand with romantic love – a home, parenting, self-love, intimacy, travel, sex and exes, soulfulness and consolation, the transformative power of sharing desires – have shown up in the songs, giving me threads to pick up and follow. At first I thought if I didn't have romantic love, these things would elude me, but then I began to see how I'd found my own ways towards them.

In each song, a particular lyric seems to direct itself to me as a question. About why romantic love is deemed essential to our ideas of the home and shared domestic fulfilment. About the choices made and not made to have children. About why romantic love can feel dependant on the ability to achieve self-love. About whether intimacy is possible in a life lived in the absence of romantic love. About how to travel and take pleasure alone. About my romantic affairs, the crazy feelings of sexual attraction, limerence, unrequited love and the strategies I deployed to numb romantic desire and rejection out of my mind. About whether the love I had for my friend Roddy had more significance than our definitions of love and relationships allowed. About what the soul means for me when I've no soulmate. About how if I've found and created meaning in my life, I might find myself transformed by what takes shape in romantic love's absence.

I've had two periods of therapy. The last time, the therapist asked me to set goals for my future. One was that I wanted a romantic partner. Even as I expressed this desire, I was mobilised by resistance: my flight response took hold in my body. 'What's going on for you, right now?' she asked me. I told her I wanted to flee. During the session, she repeatedly asked me 'what would it look like, feel like, to walk towards this fear, rather than trying to protect yourself from it?' I found myself lacking answers. 'Perhaps,' she eventually said, 'your fear is that life is OK without romantic love? Perhaps it is scary to accept you are not deficient without it.' There was some truth in that; my life wasn't bad, and I had likely become preoccupied with the stigma of being without romantic love, rather than looking at the other feelings I had towards it. Life lived in the absence of romantic love was violently at odds with how I saw myself and what I'd hoped for my future. I didn't want to be satisfied with my life as it was and I wanted romantic possibility, I wanted to understand what was keeping me away from romantic love. The last person who loved me romantically, my friend Roddy, died. I had not been able to reciprocate.

I feel moved to interrogate those feelings for myself, and for others too, because I wonder if we all lose by centring romantic love in our lives. And it does still feel like romantic love is centred. Even as the internet has helped us to find our own warm pocket of community within the endless variations of romantic and sexual identity; even though state and church control of who can and cannot be romantically and sexually involved, and who can have their relationship recognised, has loosened. Nothing has displaced romantic love from its holy status. If we were to pay attention, what do we fail to notice, share and celebrate because of this? Is it possible that life without romantic love isn't so bad? Is it possible we can take as much pleasure in other loves, find new ways of incorporating romantic feeling into our lives, assign importance to crossing over thresholds that romantic love has abandoned? All those things could be true. But if they are, is it OK to still want romantic love too? I need to know because I feel like I've got myself stuck. Entrenched in the pain of not having, but silently warring against it to present myself as OK.

I've joked to friends how this endeavour 'will put the nail in my romantic coffin for once and for all'. It scares me to lay out all the ways in which absence of romantic love touches my life. I worry that writing all this down brings the risk of damage, gives people too much information. I fear I'll end up a subject of conversation, supported by ample written evidence I have freely and elaborately provided, about why I've been without romantic love for so long. But I've tried my best not to make the question 'why am I single?' even though it is something I ask myself and have many theories about. Rather, I'm motivated by how alone I have felt in being in this situation, how ashamed, and the cruel monologuing I've subjected myself to. I know I'm not the only one feeling this way. Even though it's more unusual to live outside of the bounds of romantic relationships than it is to live within them, I feel it could be valuable to us all to think about the ways in which we can create good lives without expecting romantic love to do the work.

Yoko Ono said, 'Each time we don't say what we want to say, we're dying.' I feel those words in my whole body. So, I must speak. It might be that I will live the whole of my life attended by a sense of lack, romantic love eluding me, but I must be brave enough to say out loud, *I did want it. I do want it.* It's still possible I'll end up a victim of my own passivity, of my reluctance to expose myself to pain's potential, but admitting this is my own kind of trying, of reaching towards love. That is something. I gave up my project of romance and now decades have passed. I want to find my way back to the road.

HOME

the bed's too big, the frying pan's too wide

On the flight home from Los Angeles there was a couple in the row in front of me who shared a pillow between their two headrests and watched a film together. It moved me, in the way that feeling can flood your body sometimes, in the way absence can pour in. I was being let into a private scene and witnessed its easy intimacy. I sat there thinking of what I wish I had. Someone who would set up the film for us to watch together. Someone to refold my blanket after I'd left my seat. Someone to include me in their 'we'.

When I am cooking, I sing a line from Joni's 'My Old Man' to myself. She sings that when her lover is away from home 'the bed's too big, the frying pan's too wide'. That's what the couple sharing the pillow suggested: they seemed like the kind of couple who'd never spent a night apart, who would find the absence of the other pouring into and altering their shared domestic space. I love my empty bed; it never feels too big for me. And I've slept alone for so many years that I find it hard to share a bed these days. The frying pan on the other hand. The frying pan has an altogether different intimate quality. Perhaps it's because people so often fry eggs for someone they love. And to eat eggs together suggests a synchronised hunger, suggests sleeping and waking together, and says *please linger, please stay*. Perhaps it's the sweet balance of *you cook and I'll wash up*, how the pan moves from one person's job to another, and the ordinariness of that joint endeavour. When I'm in the home of a couple I watch for these interactions with deep interest – the routine of them – some are so tender it feels like I've taken huge gulps of yearning. I swallow them back so that I don't disclose how much I want what's theirs.

*

In my fantasy of romantic life, the private home is where I most frequently position an imagined partner. The tender exchange of one chore for the other, or companionship in remaking the bed, have stuck with me as domestic and romantic ideals. Occasionally when I prepare a meal, as I do several times most days, I resent clearing away the dishes. And sometimes when I try to get the duvet in its cover, I feel a pathetic sense of unfairness that it is only me who has responsibility for it. And when there are issues to resolve – a broken boiler, a leaking tap, an unexpected bill – I know the flaring up of my irritation and presumed helplessness is stirred not only by inconvenience but by a roaming sadness that needs a grievance to attach itself to. I have always wanted a home that felt like I wanted romantic love to feel – warm, intimate, symbolic in all the aesthetic details of it, and after the inevitable addictive whirr of lust, secure.

I did not see this ideal in my childhood homes. Ours was a household of seven – five children and my parents. When I was nine, we'd moved from Gillingham in Kent back to my dad's hometown of South Shields to a three-storey terrace, coated in pebble-dash, with a small front garden and a yard. On the ground floor was a serving hatch between the kitchen and dining room, where there was a brickwork 'bar' with hooks behind it to hang tankards. The living room had thick auburn-coloured carpet (which in the twenty years it was our family home was never replaced), and swish matching vertical blinds and curtains. The kitchen, though very small, had slatted saloon doors, which made the entrance to it seem cartoonish, and in the attic rooms there were small cupboards that you could crawl into and hide. We battled for space, dominance, our noises of choice, and peace at clashing intervals. On the second storey my younger brother Dan and I shared a room next to my parents until I began comprehensive school. On the third, my sister Rebecca had her own room and my two older brothers Matthew and Stephen shared the largest bedroom where we would all occasionally play video games. A sonic hallmark of living in that house was all of us thundering up and down the stairs.

It was vast and plush in comparison to our previous home in Gillingham, which my parents had bought in desperation when a much brighter, nicer house purchase had fallen through. My memories of Gillingham have their own turbulence. So many things were happening to our family unit, and to me, that I was too young to understand and could only experience. In the early 1980s my dad had trained to become a social worker. It led to a political awakening for him – he became a union shop steward and joined the Workers Revolutionary Party (WRP). He left the Baptist church – which was how my parents had met – and as an activist, particularly around the miners' strike, was barely at home. I think the only time I spent alone with him was when I joined him on a march, helping to sell copies of the WRP's paper *The News Line*. But I remember something of the Gillingham house. There were two rooms on each floor. Upstairs the three boys shared a bedroom and my sister and I another. The living room wall was knocked through to the hall and there was a separate room filled with boxes (probably copies of the WRP paper), which housed my dad's piano and where a poster of Lenin covered an entire wall. In the basement was the kitchen, my parents' room and, just past the kitchen, a small, cold and gloomy bathroom. For a treat, Mum would put a drop of washing-up liquid in the bathwater that my brother Dan and I shared, making it bloom with bubbles. Sometimes I would close myself into the kitchen and play the whole of Madonna's *True Blue*, making up dances to each song, in training for a future life where I dreamed I'd be a dancer. I remember one year the ceiling fell in, and next door there was an old bomb site that people dumped their rubbish into. Dad found our dining table in it. When we moved to South Shields, I thought we'd shot up in the world.

With five kids between the ages of seven and seventeen, the new house couldn't maintain a sense of grandeur once we moved our unruliness, squabbles and mess in. The aesthetic elements were disjointed. My parents didn't have a lot of money and neither did their parents, or their parents' parents. Our furniture was second-hand, not in a nicely thrifted way, but in a this-is-all-we-can-afford way. How the home looked was so far down the list of priorities for my parents, who were always 'in the red' – something I knew was bad but did not understand – and personal taste was a triviality that they could not afford to pay attention to. Consequently, I would feel in awe of other people's houses, running my fingers back and forth across the silky gold bullion fringe that trimmed their three-piece suites, pushing a fingernail into sumptuous Anaglypta wallpaper to leave a half-moon shape in it. Noticing details in my friends' bedrooms, like matching duvet sets, curtains and lampshades, child-sized wardrobes and child-sized coat hangers and chests of drawers with neatly arranged socks and underwear. Peeking into their vast fridge-freezers, with name brand soft drinks and microwaveable chips. I gradually became ashamed of our home, which felt shabby and chaotic in contrast.

In some of my friends' homes I was also able to observe married lives outside of those in my family. I realised that my parents' relationship did not appear to be a loving one. The home environment paralleled the romantic one. I once tried to will their relationship better, making a fuss of Valentine's Day on the wall calendar in the kitchen, inviting my dad to observe it. I didn't know then that he was in a relationship with someone else. That my mum knew. That his absences were not to do with work, or a twice-weekly gig playing piano in a pub, but were instead his keeping up an entirely separate intimate life.

Our home felt dictated by my dad's mood, a controlling mind that could transform the environment from calm to conflict in moments. With every opening of the front door he reset the stage to a new design, sometimes literally – turning off lights, slamming shut doors he could not tolerate being left open. If my bedroom door was ajar, he'd abruptly pull it shut as he walked past it. This has given me a lifelong startle response. There's a diary entry from that time where I wrote 'Dad's screaming blue murder again,' an expression I'd picked up from my mum. I'd sometimes feign illness, not because I wanted to avoid school, but because I wanted the experience of being home alone, of adjusting it to my own vision, of having time there without the risk of a blow-up or being disturbed from my reverie by a family member and having to accommodate them. I was desperate for my older siblings to leave home so that I could graduate into having a room of my own. I was sometimes desperate for my dad to leave too.

I remember my mum saying that, even after many years of marriage, her heart beat fast when she heard my dad walking up the path to our door. It frightened me that those feelings would extend way into adulthood. At the time I wondered if that's what love was like, a state of permanent butterflies, the superb anticipation of someone. Now I wonder if it was instead pure anxiety about whether things would be good or bad that day. My dad seemed oppressed by the family life he'd created, and I feared the anger he felt about it, the tight knot of it. Mum would say to us all, 'don't worry, his bark is worse than his bite,' but I didn't want to experience either. I can look at my dad's situation objectively and have empathy for someone who felt trapped by his domestic, familial conditions. I can also feel pride and gratitude that his politics informed mine. But of course, as his daughter, objectivity can only be fleeting. The legacy of how it felt to live with him during my childhood overrides the adult perspective I can now bring to it. Living alongside my parents' relationship encouraged in me an inclination to let male figures in my life set the tone for my relationship with them, to respond to their mood and desire rather than meet them with my own. I've so often found myself pleasing, placating, managing – perhaps thinking that this was how I needed to be to receive someone's love. The older I've become the more appalled I am by my own pliability. The situation also made me crave a place with a dependable temperament, which felt emotionally safe, knowing that in that safety love would grow.

My maternal grandparents gave this environment to us all. Their relationship was run along conventional lines – Grandma would cook, Grandad would do the washing-up.

Grandad would make the morning cups of tea to have in bed, the coffee for elevenses. At the end of each day, together they would lay the table for breakfast. When they married my grandma made a cross-stitch with a verse from the Bible: 'For wither thou goest, I will go; and where thou lodgest, I will lodge'. It wasn't that they embodied romantic love, though their hand-holding while walking down the street touched me, it was their unwavering. Once, as adults, my sister and I asked my grandma a question we would never have dared to as children: how did she put up with our grandad? He often inspired in us joshing groans of 'Grandad!' due to his bad, repetitive jokes. 'Oh, love, I guess,' she answered. What kept my grandparents 'tied and true' wasn't a passionate love of sexual compatability or even attraction, it was a love of fellowship, a shared faith and a commitment to the parts each would play in the domestic home. It's not that I wanted a relationship like theirs necessarily – I was too self-dramatising and greedy for the quiet love they had – but it was clear to me it was a basis on which you could build a good life.

They had a weekly menu they rarely diverted from. Salad on Mondays. Fish on Fridays. Roast on Sunday. I remember as a child always leaving their table satisfied, even the foods were exciting to me, things we didn't get at home: Dairylea triangle toasties, fruit yoghurts, fresh orange juice. My little brother Dan and I would stay over in half-term and every visit my grandparents would make one meal a spectacle, with me and Dan receiving our lunch in the living room armchairs, a table each pulled from the nested trio, dining at a pretend hotel. Grandma was cook; Grandad was waiter. Starter – tomato soup. Main – fish fingers and peas. Pudding – tinned fruit salad. It was the land of plenty. When I visited them as an adult, I was struck by how austere their provisions were, how small the portions, and how, were there to be any leftovers, no matter how meagre, they would be carefully wrapped and stored. Three slices of cucumber in a tiny dish, covered with foil from the top of a ready meal that had been removed, cleaned and stashed away along with the wrappers from packets of butter, which, now I think back, they so rarely had, being bound to a strict budget; margarine was what I remember being set on their table. The dishwater was thrown over the flower beds.

Not only did the customs and habits of the household remain the same, the contents did too, and this staid but harmonic environment was a source of tremendous comfort. Its crockery and cutlery enchanted me. Pyrex with matching lids, cut-glass serving bowls that caught the light, sandwich plates, faux-bone-handled knives, a special spoon for grapefruit, a special spoon to scoop a boiled egg from a pan. An egg timer filled with sand so old it could no longer keep time. Most of these were wedding gifts; some we were able to identify in a list we found after my grandparents died, a typed document Grandma had made to record who needed to be thanked for what. These objects seemed to possess an inscrutable but absolute adulthood. In the accumulation of objects that played very specific roles, I too would attain that quality – the beautiful mystery and command of having an adult place in the world. A relationship to objects that could cause me to collide with lonesomeness, where romantic love would charge the material world with symbols of the presence or absence of someone I loved. It might be their favourite jumper on the back of a chair, one I could pull on to feel close to them when they were elsewhere. A still-warm cup in the sink. Or coming home to see a light on in the hall, home's mood already animated.

Back then I read things I saw in my grandparents' home as aesthetic choices. A tablecloth on their dining table. Doilies and arm and back covers on the furniture. Now I realise the practicality of such things. The cloth saved the labour of wiping down the dining table after each meal. The arm covers on their chairs elongated the life of the furniture. The doilies and coasters kept the tables unmarked. The aesthetics of those things were irrelevant. They were simply part of my grandparents' home economics. Everything lasted and nothing was replaced.

Though it's true that I envied the order and cleanliness of the homes of my friends, I did not enjoy their uniform modernity. I've always desired a home that possessed the quality of being lived in for decades, a worn-downness, the slow accumulation and proliferation of cutlery, pots and pans. I wanted to live around handed-down things, to feel the edge of the bedspread fraying sweetly with continuous belonging, radiating cosiness. A blue Formica table and yellow curtains in the kitchen. A garden where sedums and moss would work their way into all the cracks in the boundary walls. A tin full of wonderfully odd buttons. Mirrors with their fog of age. I'd sometimes spot this kind of home in films, and I'd freeze the frame to get a picture, try to break down what within the set design had caught this essence of my grandparents' home and how I might recreate it. This was a richer fantasy for me than the idea of a wedding list, than a matching set of good plain white china. I wanted every object around me to be imbued with my story, or at the very least *a* story. I even nursed a delusion that the homes I lived in, even the ugly, cold, damp ones, loved me back, or, even more deluded, loved me most of all their inhabitants, because I had lived in them with such devotion to homemaking. Even now, I cannot walk past our old family home in South

Shields, or my grandparents' house in Deal. They are like lost loves it is still too painful to look in the eye.

*

I began to set up home early, readying myself for romance's entrance into my domestic life – an 'if you build it, they will come' mentality. I bought my first set of crockery when I was thirteen from an antiques shop in Tynemouth with £10 that I'd received for my birthday. It is still intact – coffee cups, saucers and matching plates painted with a 1970s blue circular pattern. One year I asked for a wooden hat stand for Christmas – the sort you'd see in a bistro – and was bought one from the Littlewoods catalogue. On it I hung my one velvet hat, my sister's peachy satin hand-me-down dressing gown and my hockey stick. Then I got my first chair – a 1960s black-and-white Sputnik chair from a vintage shop called Atticus in Newcastle. It cost £13 and I kept it until recently when, needing more space, I gave it away. Two young women came to pick it up for their student house and I had to stop myself from telling them how long I'd had it, how I'd loved it – resisting any attempt to control its future, to charge its atoms with my love. In my teenage bedroom with its crockery, lava lamp, hat stands (in the end there were two), chair, bedspread, I was creating a material proxy for my idea of myself and storing up things that would create a home in which the 'warm chords' of love could play.

Having acquired some household items of my own, I wanted to put them to proper use, so I started to issue invitations for dinner and afternoon tea. I am not sure where I got that idea from. Dinner in our house of seven was not ordinarily a group activity and my parents had no mutual friends to cater for. Due to the isolating nature of my mum's marriage and the demands childcare placed on her, she had no friends at all. I remember only one dinner party in my family home, when my dad had some friends over one weekend while my mum was at her union's annual conference. He instructed us not to disturb them that night and we were not introduced. I felt annoyed that I couldn't spy on how dinner parties were conducted in real life. Were there three courses? Was the wedding cutlery canteen opened for the occasion? Were they drinking wine? All I experienced of it was the drift of sound from the floor below, adult voices I did not recognise with their ebullient, exclusive chatter. It crosses my mind now that they might not even have known we existed.

Most days we would file in from school or college or work at our various hours, with our various dietary leanings, and each fend for ourselves. But one Saturday night I hosted two school friends for a 'dinner party' and cooked them a bland meal of Quorn in a cream sauce and we ate it at the dinner table listening to Ella Fitzgerald, playing bourgeoise adults. Another time my sister and I invited some girls we knew through the Newcastle riot grrrl scene for a (to my mind subversive) tea party, making cupcakes iced with flowers, spiderwebs and *grrrl power!* and sharing fanzines with one another.

In my first year at university, I didn't cook much, but once I moved from halls into a shared flat with friends, I claimed cooking as part of my identity. There was a shop close to our flat called Maumoniat International Supermarket. It sold foods I'd never seen or tried before. Halloumi. Baba ghanoush. Rice noodles. Tamari. Okra. Beautiful round porcelain-coloured aubergines. A huge array of snacks. I loved being in there, slowly progressing through each aisle, trying to take in and consider all the possibilities it offered.

I knew that food had an intimate relationship to romantic love, and so far, it hadn't been part of my experience of it. At first, I would cook meals for my housemates, confused but generous meals of curry or fajitas. These were a bit more like the meals I remember from home, us all eating quickly so we could get back to whatever was next – studying, the pub, TV. Then my friend Emily and I decided we would host a dinner party, convening all the women we knew and wanted to know better for a meal at my house. We agreed to cook two main dishes – Delia Smith's spinach and ricotta lasagne, and grilled trout with almonds. I also decided I would make a version of prawn toasts but with mushrooms instead of prawns – this was a recipe I found in a paperback student cookbook – and our friend Anwen baked whole red onions with garlic and thyme. I think there were twelve of us at that dinner table. I'd never sat around a table with so many women before. I remember the room as dark and lit with candles, and plates, wine, glasses, ashtrays over every surface. We were all different that night – more confiding, funnier, serious – when free from the gaze of men. I remember it as a moment I came into some new power as a person, at home at last. I still cook for many of those women now.

I knew instinctively that the dinner table was my forum, that it could be liberated from the family unit. That the dinner table was even improved in its liberation from the family, where in my experience it often became a stage set for conflict or avoidance, everyone itching to leave it. But with friends, I loved its revelatory potential, how the table felt like an even surface for getting to know someone, for disclosure as the evening wore on. The light of the dinner table seemed to flatter me, convert acquaintances to friends, convert friends into something the word 'friend' feels inadequate for. I could see there was an art to the giving and sharing of pleasure and care at a table, or in handing out heaped plates to be eaten from people's laps. Potential friends – potential lovers – could be wooed by making bouillabaisse, or roast potatoes, or a great fried egg sandwich; my ability to host, to provide domestic care, to cook with love, was a part of my character I took pleasure from and wanted to nurture. I could see how the dinner table allowed me to step into the light, lose the insecurities I would be fighting against if this gathering were in public. I needed to be home to be loved well.

*

After leaving home, I spent twenty-one years renting flats, and except for three years in a tiny basement flat that seemed to weep with black mould, these were all shared. In London alone, I have lived in Wandsworth, Gospel Oak, Mile End, West Ealing, Camberwell, Walworth, Peckham and East Dulwich. At first, I lived with friends from university. They were all focused on saving up to buy their own houses, a goal which seemed a fairy tale to me, so I didn't even try. Besides, I had too much debt to pay off, and it only kept growing. They were always coy about how much they were able to save, about how much help their parents had given them, inheritances that they tried to speak lightly of. I knew there wasn't something due to come my way and I would try to conceal my shock when they'd tell me they had £40,000 for a deposit, or more. By the time I was thirty, all the friends in my peer group – even those in London – were either living in homes they had bought or living with a partner while saving to buy. Even so, I tried to frame their journeys as exceptional, and mine as the norm. The place I was on in my own journey was in debt – an imposing, house-deposit-sized debt, no savings, no partner.

When I visited my friends' homes, I couldn't stop myself from projecting my visions of home into their environments. I would mentally place my ornaments on the mantelpiece, consider which of their artworks I would keep on the walls, swap their colour schemes for mine. In these spaces I felt a new discontent with my situation, how rickety it made me feel to rent, and how frustrated I was that I couldn't work my interior visions on a grander scale. I wanted my friends' domestic lives more than I wanted their relationships, or at least my desire for romantic love was displaced by my desire for their homes, which felt like a less painful thing to focus on. I thought of how hard I'd always tried to make a home. I had always pushed the boundaries of what was mine: first my bed in the shared room with my sister for which I saved my pocket money to buy a cotton bedspread from the hippy shop, then the walls around the bed, and eventually a whole bedroom, every wall and surface throbbing with my material personhood. Then I graduated to a shared house where I'd edge my things, my taste, my territory into the communal spaces, attempting a takeover. In these shared spaces, I've been a domineering force, and resented other people's stuff creeping into spaces where I carefully arranged my own.

As my friends paired off with their mortgages, renovation projects and pregnancies, I had to turn to living with strangers. My discontent that I'd fallen out of step with others my age morphed into humiliation. I felt having to share located me in an infernal adolescence, and worse, the fact that I lived with flatmates exposed my lack of a romantic partner in situations where the home came up in conversation. In those moments, I felt a bizarre shame, the kind you might feel if you're still a virgin in your twenties or don't start your periods until much later than your friends – a failure to hit an imaginary deadline for graduating into real life. At work, in almost every team I've managed, I've been the oldest and the only single person or person living in shared flats in the team. I sometimes worry if to them I am a cautionary tale.

Living with strangers brought about so much negotiation, miscommunication and mutual resentment. I don't think I was especially easy to live with, for many reasons, but certainly including the fact I had so much stuff, which meant I took up more room than was fair, and I was too emotionally brittle and anxious to deal with the reality of sharing, the political and social requests it made of me. I refused the potential and did not have the imagination for the different types of shared home it was possible to create. I suspected too that my lack of stable romantic relationships had denied me the practice I needed to talk things out and face up to domestic conflicts. In my last shared flat when someone came to view the room that was available, I said to them 'I basically want the home of a middle-class couple without the relationship.' This scared the person off. I think they thought it was a proposition. What I meant was, I wanted to always know how the shared space might be used, no unexpected visitors, I wanted my supermarket flowers fresh in the vases each week, the toilet roll always stocked up, for there to be wine on the rack. I wanted to be able to use my nice cups and plates, not feel scared someone might treat them carelessly, that they might not know they were worthy of protection. I also felt resistance to living with someone who had a partner; I didn't want to be alongside romantic love, for it to nestle in my own home, with none of it for me. I wanted the home life I'd observed in the orbit of some of the couples I knew – comfortable, predictable, somehow more adult than my own. In the absence of a partner, I knew I had to create this for myself. For the home to be able to hold me, be a place of safety for the times joy and pleasure felt withheld from me.

Now I live alone, I have created this kind of home, but I still worry. Living in a shared house, I established routines that felt necessary to guard some private space. I would take my morning coffee into bed so that I didn't get stuck having a conversation with a person before I was ready to have one. I'd watch TV mainly on my laptop, rather than the TV in the kitchen/living room, so that I wouldn't be disturbed by someone cooking a meal. I kept to a strict alarm call so that I could be certain the bathroom would be free. It has taken some time to loosen myself from these habits – but I've found I cannot deviate from my morning coffee routine, even when I am a guest in someone's house and there is an expectation of communal cafetières. I take my own steel-walled one wherever I go. Also my favourite cup. And brown sugar. And coffee.

The last time I shared a flat I began to panic as my new flatmate Bryony unloaded her belongings in the hall. She said she didn't have much stuff, I thought, stress surging through my body. In the end I loved living with her, a stranger who became a close friend, but I never got over my resistance to her things in what I privately saw as a space more mine than hers. She was like me – had accumulated the fixtures, fittings and decor of an almost-household, without the house. Both of us wanting to live alone and neither of us able to afford to. Thinking now of how closely I have guarded my shared domestic territories, I fear I might not ever be able to give an inch should I want to share a home again. A wall for a partner's record collection. A bike in the hall. A plant I find ugly.

A rite of passage – *we're moving in together* – feels remote not just because I'm single, but because I'm unsure how able I am to co-create a home, to be moderated by another's aesthetic and practical needs and wants. I don't think this unyielding creature is who I want to be.

*

Buying a home felt like a delusional dream. It wasn't just being single, only having my own resources to draw on, or the fact that there was no fat deposit waiting for me in parental bank accounts; it was my financial history. I'd taken out payday loans, had had credit card bills, more loans, an overdraft, running into tens of thousands of pounds of debt. I'd read that it would be impossible for me to get a mortgage because of this, 'payday loans kill mortgage applications' being a particular line that I'd seen and repeated to myself. I also knew I wasn't over my spending problems. When I was thirty-eight, I took redundancy from my job in the civil service and was able to clear my entire debt, but within a couple of years it had grown again, a bindweed I gave up fighting to eradicate. I had a feeling of dread for my future. At forty years old I was convinced I'd still be living in rented, shared accommodation in forty years' time, never able to choose the colour of my walls, with a clot of fear every time the landlord got in touch, and every time I needed to get in touch with them because something had gone wrong or broken, that they might take my home away from me. In my years of renting, I've paid for so many things to be fixed rather than deal with a landlord who would always be slow to respond, happy to let you live without hot water for days on end or to try to get by on the cheap with a botched job. 'You may own the flat, but this is my home,' is something I once said to a landlord, trying to get them to see things differently. The thought of living like that forever was unbearable. But within this hopelessness I must have had some faith. When I took redundancy, I had some money left over after I'd paid off the debt. I put £1,000 in a Help to Buy savings account and had been paying in £200 a month – saving for the first time in my life. I had made a commitment towards my own future, even though I hadn't acknowledged the hope this symbolised. I wasn't in the dire financial situation I had been in before, but the desire path of my self-image was so well trodden, it was hard to divert from the idea that I was a financial disaster, a hopeless case.

A few years after making that deposit, I decided to call a mortgage broker to ask about my chances. Bryony, twelve years younger than me, had told me she'd likely be moving in with her girlfriend. It made me feel peculiarly upstaged; she had her life together and was moving on into the placid, dependable world of adult life. It was no longer my peer group who had left me behind, it was people a generation my junior. I needed just one thing in my life to be fixed in place. The idea of living with another stranger was intolerable – I didn't think I'd get lucky again like I had with Bryony. The broker I spoke to was very relaxed, frighteningly casual even, with the squeaky voice of a very young man. He told me it would probably all be fine, as long as my debts were cleared, as long as the payday loans were a few years old. He said I could probably get a mortgage on my salary if I could raise the 5 per cent deposit. I started to piece together how to make that happen and realised that if I kept saving for another couple of years, I might have the money I needed to buy a flat. When this became a concrete possibility, it turned out that while my parents couldn't make big contributions, they could both chip in a thousand pounds, and my grandad, after chatting to my mum, said he'd give me what he planned to leave me in his will. Together they helped nudge me to the 5 per cent I needed a year sooner than I might have done alone. Something I believed out of reach, that would be denied, was now a present reality. I would get the chance to make a home for myself. I feel some guilt that I too in the end 'had some help' like the people I'd always resented. I wish things were different, that there were other ways to find secure housing and the freedom to arrange a domestic life to your own designs.

In October 2019 I bought a one-bedroomed flat in a low-rise block in New Cross. In the months leading up to the sale going through, I began to buy small items for it. I stored them in a large aluminium trunk, as though it was a marriage chest. In it I placed vintage Irish linen tea towels I'd been collecting from charity shops, a set of plain white enamel bakeware, some brand-new sharp kitchen knives, a bottle of Aesop hand soap I'd used once in a nice bar, a pair of 1950s Heals curtains from eBay, a rose-scented candle, a circular framed embroidery from the 1970s. Every now and then I'd look in the chest and think of how it would feel to locate these things in a place called mine. This feeling was serene. I'd been soothed.

I needed that: all throughout the process of buying the flat I felt afraid that something would go wrong, that I would be humiliated at the last moment – rejected by the elaborate fuck you of house-buying bureaucracy. At the time I kept thinking about a degrading rejection I'd experienced. A man I was sleeping with had stayed over. I saw him to the door, and he couldn't stop kissing me, he stood there laughing, saying 'oh my god I can't stop kissing you, I have to go! I have to go!' Eventually he left and I remember closing the door behind me, my body ringing like a golden bell, a smile across my entire face. A few minutes later I received a text from him, telling me *nothing can happen between us, I don't feel that way about you*. It was a cruel and shocking contrast in emotion. I've been on guard ever since.

The day I got the keys to my flat, I entered it alone, and at first felt the sadness of a home that is empty of all that makes it one. The sounds I made walking through the rooms, opening cupboards and doors, my feet on the laminated wood floor, clanged unpleasantly. The flat was gloomy with the residue of otherness in the smell and texture of the rooms, the vanishing of the life of it. I needed people. That evening, a small group of friends came by. I ordered us pizza, which we cut into slices with scissors, and we drank champagne from fine flutes etched with daisies that I had stashed away for this moment. I hadn't moved in yet but being in the flat with my friends for a few hours was a kind of spell I wanted to place on it before my two cats and I settled within its walls. Through this opening up, right from the start, I would establish my home as a place not just for me, but for everyone I loved, and might come to love. My mum arrived the next day and she and I painted the living room and my bedroom, joined by my best pal Becky and Bryony. As they painted alongside me, jobs divided up and walls completed through collaboration, I felt they were layering on something more than colour. I decided to interpret it as an infusion of care into the walls that would hold me.

*

I had adopted two kittens in 2013, the first time I lived alone in that mouldy flat in Peckham. I was very depressed then, reeling from the involvement with the man who had not been able to stop kissing me, who had left me cowed and stunned at my undoing. One day I'd had the back door open, and a stranger cat wandered in. The cat climbed up onto my sofa and walked along the back of it, tightrope style, and spent a few minutes allowing me to pet it. The flat suits a cat, I thought to myself, amused. With the entrance of this cat, I experienced such a joyful disruption of my mood, I felt entirely diverted from whatever had been causing me to suffer in that moment. And so, a couple of months later I brought two kittens home with me. The integration of care for them into my daily life felt like a rescue. I could still experience loneliness, I could enjoy and guard the pleasure of solitude, but I was never utterly alone. The presence of the cats, the ability to communicate through touch, through body language, brought a new texture to my life, an emotional and physical richness that would not be there without them. But it is its own unique sensation, and I respect and value it for its itselfness, not as a proxy for human-to-human connection. I knew when I moved into my flat in New Cross that seeing them explore the rooms, watching them find and take up new positions of comfort and perches to survey their territory, would make me feel happy, would make me at home. Joni had two cats in her Laurel Canyon house too.

*

I have lived in my flat for two and a half years now. I have those things I so wanted when I was a child: a set of twelve holly-patterned hors d'oeuvre dishes Roddy bought for me that only come out at Christmas, a punchbowl with matching cups, old cotton napkins, a special pot for honey, a special dish and spoon for jam. I have multiple sets of bed linen, sherry glasses, spare duvets and light bulbs, guest towels, vases of every size and colour, tools, first aid supplies, nice soap at each sink. I am ready, I am prepared for maintaining my own comfort and creating it for others. I have many of my grandparents' dishes, glasses and trinkets, including a holiday-in-Winchester souvenir chopping board, a wooden-handled fish slice with the yellow and green paint worn away and a hammered metal sea-green stapler. I am flanked by objects, each with a story. I sometimes worry it's a kind of oppression, this responsibility I feel towards the safekeeping of these stories. But that feeling always passes: the pleasure of my things, being around my dependable things, is too great.

Creation of my private domestic space is a kind of romance: aesthetically speaking, I wear my heart on my sleeve. Minimalism disturbs me, leaves me guessing: what does this sparse person love, and who? I layer colour, texture, pattern and, like loading a plate at a buffet, I'm not too worried about what goes with what. I go through long-term devotions to colour: yellow, blue, and pink and green together. Each of these phases has an origin object or setting. Yellow grew from a birthday gift: a sunshine-yellow old-fashioned Roberts radio. Blue evolved from the rented flat I lived in, its pale blue living room and the bedroom I slept in, which was white but with a blue floral wallpapered border and blue ceramic handles on the wardrobe. The pink and green walls, bed linen and furniture in my flat come from a vintage paisley-patterned quilt my sister bought me for Christmas. These colours became a kind of organising principle around which to arrange my aesthetic life. Often that didn't mean buying lots of new things, it meant bringing to the fore a glass jug or candlestick or book cover that seemed in harmony with my new romantic interest. But this falling for colour evolved so subtly – I wouldn't notice I was in a phase until the dressing of a room spoke of it.

I feel I'm on the move into a new phase, one that is enamoured with the in-betweenness of blue and green. It was seeded during my trip to Los Angeles, when I saw blue/green everywhere, and since I returned, I've found myself acknowledging the occurrences of blue/green around my rooms, in the garden, other colours remaining present but receding from my mind's eye. A drawing in felt tip that I'd bought from the artist Penny Goring years ago took on a new significance, its wet slate and electric colours calling. A single art nouveau tile, decorated with a pink chrysanthemum on a turquoise background, with furling green foliage in varying tones. Two hand-painted linen cushions I've had for a while, one blue, one green, but each containing the other colour. From my friend Amanda I bought a pair of small paintings, one with a blue mood, one with a green mood. Blues and greens unwilling to commit to be either one or the other, dwelling in a space of bothness. I realise I've wanted to enclose myself within this state of possibility to activate an environment – a mood – that not only might support my own change and growth but somehow also induce it. On some level, I think this creation of cosiness, the security and splendour of my setting is where my creative impulses find the confidence to step forward, make me take notice of them, spur me to act. This might be what the *right* home and *right* romantic love share – a stable point from which it is possible to make a scary jump.

Having people over has become as integral to my sense of self as writing, music and being in the water. Every year I host a Christmas party, planning it and accumulating supplies over several months just like my mum used to do – forbidding us access to the nuts, snacks and chocolates that slowly grew in the run-up to Advent. I make invitations and design a menu. I bulk order cheap cava or prosecco or crémant, buy brown sugar cubes and Angostura bitters to make 'champagne' cocktails. I roll up the rug and hide it away, move the furniture to enable the best flow of people in my small flat, ease for the smokers who will want to frequently nip outside, places for people to rest their drinks. I love the few minutes before my guests arrive and I've arranged everything just how I like – a tablecloth, my prettiest glasses for water and for wine, candles lit, cold cold fizz in the fridge. I always buy wine glasses from charity shops because the glasses are always at risk of being smashed. Some parties everything survives intact, others there is smash after smash after smash. I embrace these conventions of grown-up hosting. When the first guests arrive, usually my hair is still wet as I've spent too long getting the flat ready and left too little time for getting myself ready. But it doesn't matter, I have a sense that it's how the house feels when people enter it – the 'warm chord' of the house – that will make them feel loved.

Anyone who eats at my table is loved there – and I confess to feeling relieved that I don't find myself preparing meals for people I might only consider an obligation. I don't have to perform as someone's partner with the joint diary, the tit for tat of mutual social upkeep. I try to think of the kitchen as a theatre of self-creation. Sometimes it's as simple as putting pickles in a pretty dish and laying the table. Or slicing up fruit and arranging it on a plate that makes the colours vibrate. Other times it's the rejection of restraint when cooking for one. I always feel defensive when people say 'I don't bother when it's just me.' It's not that I don't value convenience and simplicity – I love supermarket tortellini and instant noodles as much as anyone – but I infer from their words that they don't think I am worth it. I'm not saying that cooking myself a five-pan, six-hour meal is a radical act, but it says my pleasure is worth investing in, is worth putting love into, even if I don't always believe that, even if sometimes I feel profligate, greedy, unsatisfied.

Still, as much as I take seriously the cooking of meals just for myself or to eat with others, every so often I think of peaceful meals between two people who are in love with an ache that seems perilously close to my skin. I yearn for someone to get gently, sleepily drunk with on my sofa. I miss how Roddy and I were able to lean on each other to fulfil that need for a mild domestic love we both wanted. I want quiet abandon, to feel unguarded. I crave the peculiar familiarity of someone who'd be enchanted by my blocked pores, the erosion of bodily shame. Friends who share houses and flats say to me, 'Oh, it must be so nice living alone, you can walk around naked.' I'm still uncomfortable walking around naked partly because there is no one to see that I am naked. Sometimes when I pick up a glass of wine, or walk across the living room, I imagine being watched by someone who loves me. I find myself trying to look sweet, or sexy, or hoovering comically for the benefit of another. Then I catch myself. I spill my wine, I trip on the rug, yank the hoover's plug from the wall by accident. My performance is ridiculed by the absence of an audience. I love to live alone, but I long to know I'm real beyond my own comprehension. It's not just intimacy I long for, it's that pact some couples have, the one I saw at work in my grandparents' relationship. I want to excuse myself from solving a problem because *that's not my area*, to trade off my skills against a partner's, to feel I compensate for lack in one area with strength in another. I don't enjoy the feeling of complete responsibility. My resentment reveals itself in how I tackle tasks that I don't perceive as 'mine'. Wonky shelves are put up and tolerated, correction of my mistakes seemingly beyond me.

I know there is another dynamic, one where there isn't equity, where certain labours are women's work; that my notion of harmonic, collaborative domesticity is idealised. Even though I identified an equilibrium in my grandparents' relationship, I know that for many years, before I was born or was old enough to notice, my grandmother's role was to keep house and arrange all domestic activities around my grandad's work and my mum's childcare. My grandma was very intelligent and during World War II she had worked in a government office in Whitehall. When she married, like so many women of her generation, she retreated to the home while my grandad worked. One of the surprising things we came to learn after she died was that she had wanted to be a pharmacist – I'd given her a book to write in with prompts like 'How did you meet my grandad?' and 'What did you want to be when you grew up?' When I'm in one of my family's domestic spaces or away with friends, I pick up gendered labour as naturally as the line of women I come from. I take charge, plan and cook the meals, feed children, keep things tidy. I find it embarrassing how much credit I give men who play their part in this – it's so novel. I also notice the rare woman who leaves all this stuff to other women in the group. She impresses me but I disapprove of her too, so internalised is this. Living alone I rarely engage in domestic cold wars or full-on battles – for the distribution of cleaning duties, for who gets to watch what on the TV, whose necessity for noise is deemed superior to the other's need for quiet, and vice versa.

My grandparents had some pale blue milk glass bowls I remember eating puddings from. They were designed for prunes and had prune-stone-shaped impressions around the rim labelled 'tinker, tailor, soldier, sailor, rich man, poor man, beggar man, thief'. The idea was to eat the prunes and place the stones in the indentations. My grandma told me it would predict who I would marry. We didn't eat prunes so I would place pips from oranges, or tinned mandarin segments. I remember the mild jeopardy of playing this game – how might life turn out for me? Tinker always appealed to me, the way the word sounded, like a fork tapping a crystal glass to make it resound. Could I love a beggar? I thought I could, unpleasantly pleased with myself. But comfort comes – my grief for romantic lack is quelled by having a home that is mine. A home that I love, and might love in. Having a home felt as remote as having a romance does now, but it happened.

In one of my early poems, I wrote 'tonight pours into your absence'. I think of the night of that poem, so wildly vast, with no boundary to contain my longing. But there was no 'you' subject I had in mind. When there's a 'you', there is lonesomeness. When there is no 'you', that is loneliness. I conjured a 'you' to summon the pleasure of longing for a specific person. I, too, sometimes note the un-slept-on pillow beside me and reach across it as though I could touch the imprint left by someone's head. *Come home*, I think, with tightness in my body like how children screw up their eyes to focus on a wish. *Come home to me.* I feel stupid and puny with my longing. I remember kisses, not a particular person's kisses, just the sensation of being kissed, a soap bubble inside of me, swelling, luminous, then gone, its phantom effect broken. *Come back*, I think. My lips fuzzy as though I've eaten something I love but am mildly allergic to.

*

Recently an estate agent visited my flat to give me a valuation. I've been thinking about moving to the coast, or, if I can swing it, somewhere in London with a garden I can plant into. My flat is 53 square metres. You can do a tour of every room in under a minute. The agent said to me, 'I love what you've done to the place!' (They'd sold it to me two years before.) I beamed. She said, 'You have a real eye – do you do this for a living?' I tried to conceal how it made me feel. I love to be praised for how my flat looks. It's a pride I allow. For days afterwards I replayed her words, not even caring that she was selling to me, wanting me to choose her to sell the flat on, to win the commission. I found it interesting to observe this about myself. When I am praised about other things, objections crowd out any compliments that have been offered. But how I arrange my home, what I choose to put in it – people noticing that and remarking on it – strikes within me a gong that radiates gratification. Every time a woman – for it is most often a woman – says 'oh, I'd love to have colour on the walls' or 'I love that pattern, but my boyfriend would never let me' I feel a swell of pleasure that I don't have to contend with the aesthetic veto of 'the other half'. At least in my situation I haven't had my taste neutralised into an unthreatening, benign palette by the need for compromise. This allows my dreams for a potential future home to be uninhibited, to know I might – budget aside – indulge every fussy and prim little detail of my fancy.

Rooms (and it must be rooms, not the blank expanse of open-plan living) painted the colours of blue hydrangeas, yellow municipal park tulips, verdigris, pink praline, tinned custard, glaucous leaves, the frail colour of daylight as you emerge from a cave. The rooms would have names. Wallpaper found beneath other layers of wallpaper, patterned lino found beneath carpet, parquet floors, old stained-glass. Little twin candle lights fixed to the wall either side of the bed. A chintzy curtained cupboard beneath a big white porcelain sink. An emporium of table lamps with simple silk shades. A brick-walled garden. An intricate mosaic floor depicting my cats in a classical design. Roses lining the path, wisteria, acers, fleabane. A wrought-iron Juliet balcony. A natural swimming pond. Bevelled overmantel mirrors. An armoire with my long dresses floating from padded hangers. A bathroom covered in pale green, white and pale pink tiles, like a perfect prawn cocktail – the enormous bathtub with steps leading up to it. A larder. Ceiling-to-floor antique lace curtains. A Wurlitzer. A large table reserved for doing jigsaws. In every room at least one comfortably upholstered chair – velvet, silk, ticking, brocade. A huge linen press filled with bed sheets, tablecloths, napkins and blankets that have been washed and dried repeatedly, so they are as soft as cats' ears. And surfaces everywhere – shelves, sconces, cupboards, plinths, windowsills, nooks on which to arrange all the things I love. I want the house to provide a spectacular assault course for my cats, so I can watch their descent from bookcase, to cabinet, to chair back, to table, to sofa, to my lap and back again, as though they're playing a game of Floor Is Lava. I realise the house I want is large. I know that's greedy. I realise in thinking about this house with its wooden stairs that I want them to become worn, a slight dip in their centre, by all the people I love climbing up and down them.

And another dream integral to home. My dad, who joined the Royal Marines Band Service when he was fourteen, had an old upright piano, which was quite out of tune. He played it beautifully. Sometimes I'd fall asleep hearing him play 'Clair de Lune' downstairs, and I wanted to understand how it worked. When I was very young, I made up my first song on it, and devised a system for remembering: felt-tip marks on the keys I pressed. I hadn't thought at the time about how this system would not help me to remember the order in which I should press the keys, or in what rhythm. The marks I made were in a dark green colour, the green a child would choose to colour in a tree, a green that winter would not fade. I'd sometimes open the lid of the piano and remove the covering beneath the keys, exposing its workings. I loved the smell of the dust and the strings, which made my mouth taste of coins when I put my face close to them. The piano held within it an alchemical quality. I had a sense that when I had fully grown up my home would have to include a piano. The cats would sleep on top of it as I played, enjoying the vibrations of the strings.

I think back to Joni. In 'My Old Man' Joni sings of feeling able to break from convention – how, unlike my grandparents, she doesn't need to be married to keep her 'tied and true'. In living alone, I also break (if only gently) from convention. In not having a partner, or having children, I break a little further away. The ability to have a home that is shaped entirely around my needs runs in opposition to what society understands as a home, as in a family home, as in a place where women, typically, care for children and men. A home where the heart is is a family home. While my home has been created to meet my needs, one of those needs is that it welcomes, can provide comfort to, delight even, anyone who steps into it. There's an interview on Joni's website where she talks about her home in LA and her art. She says, 'I enjoy living with it. It's very personal – my friends, my cats, my antiques.' I don't need or expect to find similarities between Joni and me, but it always delights me when I do.

I love that on the wall in my bedroom there are scratches in the paintwork, where my cats have clawed the wall to steady their jump down from a high perch. That in the garden, my potted roses were staked by Becky. A red wine stain on a cushion and scented candles burning courtesy of Jane. That when my pal Crispin comes over, he walks straight in rather than ringing the doorbell. In my fridge, there is always beer, because my friends bring and leave their leftovers there for next time we get together. That without my asking, Al and Richard will take out the rubbish when they leave. Sometimes, when I have topped up all the cats' water glasses, plumped up the pillows on the sofa and switched on the lamps in each corner of the flat, a friend due to join me for dinner that evening, I feel like a peach resting on a velvet plinth – nothing could ever bruise me. My home is a family home too.

CHILD

child with a child, pretending

I don't have a habit of recording my dreams, but I had one at sixteen about having to care for an aborted baby that was so horribly visceral I wrote about it in my diary, adding that I could 'never get pregnant because I can't have an abortion now'. Three years later I did, without giving it a moment's thought. I feel the immense privilege of being able to make that decision, more acutely today than ever. I had the legal right. I did not have to pay for it. I did not feel shame. I also assumed that there would be many more chances for parenthood when conditions for it were more favourable. I knew I could not be a 'child with a child'. I felt sorrow, but I did not feel conflict.

When I was teenaged, getting pregnant was the worst thing, aside from a death, that I could imagine happening. It was the 1990s, and the media and politicians were deranged by teenage pregnancies. It seemed like newspapers were on a scavenger hunt to find the youngest mums and dads, the most dispossessed and state reliant. Once found, they would interview them, their reporting saturated with condescension and repulsion about their homes, appearances, education, relationships, accents, employment status. In the mindset of the ruling class, a pregnant child is a delinquent child, with delinquent motivations, regardless of all the things that might have contributed to that child becoming pregnant.

I remember a *Daily Mirror* report on 'Britain's Youngest Mum', about a girl who became pregnant at eleven years old. I found it online recently to remind myself of the details. At the end of the article, which fired a shot at its subject and her mother in every line, there was a message to the reader: 'ARE YOU, or is your daughter, a gymslip mum?' It asked readers to call in on a free-phone number to share their story. They were also invited to share what they felt about the girl's 'plight'. It was clear from reading the comments they printed that only certain people deserved to have a baby. One woman commented: 'I've been crying all day. [Her] story made me so angry. My husband and I have been trying for a baby for twelve years. It seems so unfair.' Another said, 'Girls from that background should be put on the pill when their periods start.'

Teenage parents are still a powerful symbol of immorality, a threat to the aggressively policed notion of what constitutes a family. Even though I intuited my early awareness of this as sexist, classist and weirdly fetishising (the label of 'gymslip mother' being charged with discomforting arousal), it was hard to fight against the idea that early motherhood was the most ruinous act, one that scuppered all future potential for both parent and child. When a girl at school became pregnant, my friends and I discussed it with solemnity, borrowing the judgement and words of adults, *what a terrible terrible waste!* When on King Street in South Shields – the main shopping street – I saw girls my age pushing a pram, usually accompanied by their mums, I would look away. I was frightened they might see the judgement on my face, and a little disgusted by how curious I was as to how the Teen Mum was handling it all. In another newspaper interview I'd read the teen mother was quoted as saying 'I just wanted something to love.' Wanting something to love made absolute sense to me.

In this context, the song 'Little Green' seemed agonisingly tender and noble. In the 1960s, when Joni became pregnant, safe, legal abortion was not available. Raising children outside of marriage was not acceptable. Joni did not want to ruin her child's life, or her own, so she relinquished Baby Green to adoption, but only after sending her into the world with the love and wisdom of the song. I nodded sagely to the lyrics, believing I would have made the same choice as Joni. No matter how much I yearned for the experience of unconditional love, I would have borne the pain of giving her up. Even consideration of this made me feel closer to the idea of womanhood I felt destined for. I sensed my womanhood would be filled with sacrifice, but it would also be beautiful, be memorable, and I would be made through my valour. It's only now I notice that 'Little Green' is *Blue*'s only lyrical address in the third person. For all *Blue*'s reputation as confessional, this story of loss needed to be protected from the immediate scrutiny that Joni's *I* voice might have brought her.

It was when I was nineteen, pushing hard against the 'teen mother' category, that I became pregnant. I was in my first year of university and my boyfriend and I had only known each other for a few months. Even so, this happening to me, to us, felt like a kind of mystical tethering: we'd made something together. Going through a difficulty with a romantic partner was what it was all about, right? This was what Joni had warned me about when she sang 'All I Want', when she said I might hate and love at the same time; it's what I'd prepared for.

I made the decision to have an abortion before I even took the pregnancy test. It would be more accurate to say I didn't even make a decision; I just knew what I'd do. By then I'd forgotten the fear and censure that early dream had struck in me. I did the test in my halls toilet, tucking it up the sleeve of my top between the toilet and my room, like I would do with a tampon so people wouldn't see – I found anything bodily shameful. I waited longer than necessary before turning the test over to look at the result and seeing it was positive. I cried a little, my boyfriend sitting on my bed with me, both of us unsure how to behave. Uneasy with what we now knew in the containment of my small room, we decided to go to the student bar, if only to be around people and not stuck with the lousy responsibility of the other's reaction. The next day I got an appointment to confirm the result at my GP and to request an abortion.

I had learned I was pregnant in early March, but my abortion was scheduled for mid-April. During that time my body rapidly changed. I outgrew my bras. I was either pale or flushed. I outgrew my jeans. I often had diarrhoea or cramps or nausea – all of which I connected to the pregnancy, rather than stress. I drank a lot (after all, it didn't matter) but found I couldn't stomach smoking anymore. I thought this crisis we shared – being pregnant – had to mean something. I thought, love meant pain, right? I had only told a handful of people, so I clung to my boyfriend. I had an image of myself as stoic during this time, but my stoicism was all surface. My boyfriend was sweet, but I could sense a bewilderment and resentment on his part, an *I didn't sign up for this* rejection of my bodily undoing and how it infringed on that liberatory year entering the world of adults. I felt it all too, but tried to pretend it wasn't affecting me in any negative way. I attempted to act as though things were the same as before, where our concerns were the interesting new friends we'd made, drinking and getting high, whether we could get cash-back in the pub even though our bank accounts were empty, fucking all night, having big, big thoughts about the world.

On the day of the appointment my boyfriend and I took a taxi to the hospital on the outskirts of Leeds city centre. When we arrived, I had to get changed out of my clothes and into a hospital gown. They'd told me to bring a dressing gown and I remember feeling embarrassed that my dressing gown and sash were mismatched, as though I'd dressed inappropriately for the occasion. It was my gown, my boy-friend's sash. Baby blue and racing green.

I waited in the cubicle alone, lying on the bed with all the contrasting blues of the sheets, lino floor, the curtain pulled around me. I listened to the women in nearby cubicles talk-ing to the nurse. I overheard what would happen to me three or four times before I heard the nurse tell me directly. They would insert a pessary into my vagina to help open the cer-vix and then a little while later I'd be taken into theatre where they would put me to sleep. When it was over, they'd wake me up and give me a drink and a biscuit. Assuming everything was OK, I would be able to go home that after-noon. The woman in the next bed had a man with her, and from what I could glean from their conversation, they'd had an affair and she was distraught at her decision. I felt relief not to be in her situation but indignant because I'd thought we weren't allowed to bring in our partners and I didn't want to be by myself, as though I didn't have someone there that loved me.

When it was my turn, I was taken into theatre where the sur-gical team were listening to 'Hello' by Oasis, loudly, and as

I was told to count backwards in my head while the anaesthetic took effect, I remember feeling angry that the procedure seemed so trivial to them that this music was deemed OK. I don't remember if I was told what they would do when I was asleep – how they would make me not pregnant. I wonder if it was a deliberate omission, or whether I closed my ears to it, resisting that detail. But I do remember my sister's then partner saying to me once, when the subject of my abortion came up, 'all they do is mash it up and suck it all out.'

After, when my boyfriend and I got back to our halls of residence, he made me crumpets. He buttered them and spread them with Marmite and placed slices of cheddar on top. We lay in bed watching TV on my ancient black-and-white set, the kind with a circular aerial you had to fuss with to get a good picture. I recalled a couple of months earlier, before I'd known I was pregnant, we were lying in bed in much the same way. My boyfriend had been asleep, and I was watching the 1960s film *Up the Junction*, based on the book of short stories by Nell Dunn. The film follows a bored rich girl who, desperate to experience what she considers to be real life – a life where people say what they want – leaves her comfortable situation to work in a factory. She becomes friends with two sisters, one of whom, Rube, becomes pregnant and has an illegal abortion. I found the film upsetting but for reasons that were oblique to me. I woke my boyfriend up crying. He asked what was wrong. 'I don't know,' I said, 'just my heart feels bad.' I remember wondering – that night after the abortion – why had I cried then, seemingly for no reason, but not now? Not crying surprised me. I felt as though I'd crossed over into a new, more knowing, less inviting territory of adulthood. At the same time, I felt babyish tucked into my single bed, in clean pyjamas.

This feeling of crossing over stayed with me. I couldn't regain my previous self. My body seemed, and looked, it felt to me, permanently altered. The slip of myself forever gone. I began to feel deeply insecure. I dyed my hair from blonde to dark brown, having internalised something my boyfriend had said about brunettes. I started eating only rice cakes. Bought clothes I couldn't afford, plundering my overdraft. Alert to anything that was deficient in me, my easy-goingness spent.

Our relationship didn't make it to a year. He broke up with me shortly after I had to go into hospital again to have a large cyst – called a Bartholin cyst – at the entrance to my vagina removed. It was found when I went to have my first cervical smear test, about four months after the abortion. Just before she inserted the speculum, the nurse casually said, 'oh look you've got a cyst there the size of a grapefruit!' as if it were an interesting feature of the landscape she wanted to draw my attention to. We'd just moved out of our neighbouring halls into a houseshare with a couple of friends, but already out of love with me and back in love with his ex, he refused to accompany me to the appointment, saying 'it's all just been too much.'

I felt wretchedly alone at the hospital when awaiting this surgery, as the consultant brought four medical students to look at the cyst before I went in. I felt even more alone when, while I was in the bath a week or so after, I had to slowly pull away the mesh that had been used to close the wound, at the direction of the doctor. Our student flat bathroom was grim, cold and fetid with mould. The mesh looked like a small piece of the metal grid you find on a disposable barbeque. It was agonisingly painful. Scraps of my skin came away with it.

At the time I thought the 'too much' my boyfriend felt was the emotional toll of being with me, unable to cope with feelings that were outsized compared to what everyone else was experiencing. But since, I've been dogged by thoughts that it was how my thrillingly fuckable body was recast as mutable, harbouring unpleasant growths. A body of risk that alarms, not entices. I had to contend with the thought that rather than desirability, I inspired an albeit regretful (he wasn't unkind) disgust. I had been socialised to expect that once I entered middle age, but at nineteen it spun me off course into a field of sorrow I could not name. I wasn't the understated and noble Joni of 'Little Green', singing softly, rearranging her sadness into a pretty, harmonic song. I felt an operatic sadness that no one would afford me a stage for. I became the girl at parties who unfailingly gets the most drunk and cries and discloses her pain to anyone who will listen, searching for other women who had done the same as me, so we could grieve our strange loss together. It was comforting that they were not hard to find.

*

The sadness I felt wasn't for the loss of a baby, for me at least, it was the discovery that I couldn't trust my body to look out for me because biology had an agenda of its own. I also resented how marked my body felt by such a short-lived pregnancy. As I got older, I felt this wasn't something I was allowed to say, as I met more and more women who were struggling to get pregnant, or who were suffering baby loss, who described their bodies as going against them. I knew how I felt was subservient to their feelings, that while I could identify with their loss and longing, articulating that to them would be obscene and insensitive. Intentional loss being a false equivalence. But it was my first experience of lamenting 'what might have been', and from that point onwards there was always a parallel existence in my mind, one where I had made a different decision. The child was present in that imagining, but no other details of life formed around it.

I had a lot of sex in my twenties but no relationships with a status that made me secure in my romantic present or future. I used a hybrid of methods to prevent pregnancy, often needing to buy the morning-after pill, or self-administer a big dose of leftover contraceptive pills (I'd read online that five pills was equivalent to the morning-after pill). I didn't always have the confidence to insist my sexual partners wore condoms and in fact I did not like using condoms, but as I didn't have a real boyfriend or partner, being on the pill full-time did not make sense to me and I was blasé about STDs. During this time, I assumed I'd eventually have a long-term romantic relationship. I took it for granted that if I waited long enough, it would happen, but I did not make the same assumption about having children. I had an instinct that my having polycystic ovary syndrome had (biologically speaking) likely wrecked my chances. But I also knew the older I got, the less likely it would be that I'd meet a man who would want to raise children with me. They might already have children of their own. They might see me as an in-between relationship before they met a younger woman who tipped their switch from not wanting to have kids to suddenly having them. Ruling out children as a given made things feel simple. I enthusiastically received news of pregnancies, wrote poems to celebrate the births of friends' children, gently held their newborns, played peek-a-boo. It had nothing to do with me, so it didn't touch any agitated, wanting part of my psyche.

I was at the births of my sister's children. The first, Elsie, was born a day into labour, and because it had gone on so long my sister had to have a surgical delivery rather than the natural birth she had hoped for. The second, Gene, I watched being born in a rush of blood, holding a lamp at a midwife's instruction above my sister as she gave birth in a pool at her home. I was embarrassed at how squeamish it made me, needing to leave the room to be sick at one point. I loved Elsie and Gene immediately with a startlingly intense love. It made me believe I would devote every second to their safety and happiness.

I remember the first night my niece was at home, listening to her crying endlessly, and getting up at 4 a.m. to enter my sister's room. I took Elsie from her arms and told my sister to sleep; she mouthed *thank you* at me. I sat on the sofa, holding Elsie, who felt light as a kitten, and did my best to soothe her. I knew I would not necessarily be able to stop her crying, but I also knew my sister and her partner had to get some sleep, there was a desperate look in their eyes. A few years later, when my sister was downstairs, in labour with Gene, I tried to get Elsie to sleep again. She could hear my sister breathing and moaning through her contractions, and Elsie kept saying to me 'what's that noise, what's that noise?' I told her it was her brother coming to meet her.

This intimate experience of witnessing childbirth and being present in the earliest days of a life was extraordinary. I felt a sense of intense responsibility, and the pleasure of love blooming in me, fast – like the shock of blood in the birthing pool when Gene was born. But I did not become a convert, did not feel these experiences switch me from *OK not to have children* to *desperately need to have children*. I held within me a mild, almost comforting channel of neutrality that I could draw on whenever I was confronted with either a direct question about having children, or other people's pain and joy in relation to that same question. I felt lucky to have escaped baby panic, that I'd somehow overrun the settings of my biology, which almost everyone told me I'd be faced with sooner or later, eluded the anguish of decision-making.

So it was a shock when I woke up the day after my thirty-seventh birthday feeling a full-bodied desire and urgent need to have a child. I do not have a close relationship with certainty, so this was a highly unusual state of mind, and though I felt tremendously excited and motivated by this change in feeling, I felt surprised, too, that my desire had raced ahead and I'd only just caught up. It wasn't a feeling that I could intellectualise, it seemed to radiate from a new influence within me – something organic and obscure, but persuasive.

There wasn't time to wait for the possibility of romantic love to present me – *ta dah!* – with a baby. I had to make plans immediately. It was liberating to unhitch myself from my desire for romance, subordinated in the face of this new compelling desire. First, I told people of my intent. 'I am going to try to have a baby,' I said. 'Will you support me?' I asked. I did this formally, by message, so that I did not have to face people's immediate reaction. 'I need to find a sperm donor,' I said. 'I need to make an appointment at a clinic.' I made an appointment. I read anything I could find online from women who'd made the same choice. There were personal essays, illustrated with joyful photos of the author and their child, group features in women's mags that listed each woman's name, age and job title; elaborate threads deep in Mumsnet, all with the same refrain – *it will be the hardest thing you ever do, but the best too*. I enlisted their experiences and stories of eventual success to help sustain me. And to be pragmatic, I also searched for stories from women who did not have children but had wanted them, to see how they resolved and lived alongside their longing. I can't remember finding any.

I waited three months to see a private fertility doctor, taking a recommendation from the friend of a friend who'd had a baby following treatment there. Before my consultation with her I had a 3D scan to look at my uterus and assess my egg situation. The doctor told me my ovaries looked OK in terms of numbers of follicles that release eggs, but that they couldn't guarantee their quality. That I needed to have a polyp removed from my uterus – the NHS probably wouldn't cover that, she said. That I would have to pay for a special kind of X-ray where they would inject a dye into my uterus to check if my fallopian tubes were clear. That in numbers terms, the odds were highly stacked against me. I left the appointment undeterred, completely consumed by a debate I was having in my head about how to ethically choose a sperm donor.

Deciding on a donor seemed sprung with traps that heteronormative romantic intent, or at least sexual attraction, could outmanoeuvre. Fancying someone gives you momentum. Instinct and impulsiveness and alcohol can propel you forward, determine your move. But in this situation, I felt detained by choices. On the UK's biggest online sperm bank you are invited to select preferences on the front page – race, eye colour, height, hair colour – as though selecting 'your type'. It's hard not to input your preferences in the same way you might on a dating site. Some people suggest selecting a donor who might offer the best chance of a child who physically resembles you. But in selecting a donor you are warned not to consider physical features alone. What about the traits you might like your child to inherit? Is it important to you that the donor is educated to a particular level? Each question forcing an evaluation of residual prejudices and assumptions I have acquired, and a hierarchy of attributes I value. So – emotional intelligence over education, height over eye or hair colour. I felt it grotesque that I considered it might be possible to correct what I saw as imbalance in my own physical features and character. Could selection of the right donor prevent a child of mine feeling sad about their 'bad legs', their short neck, propensity for moles, their poor spatial awareness? All features my parents apologised for – *sorry you've got that from me*, anything I disliked about myself accepted as objectively negative. It made it easy to assume my parents didn't like what they saw in me either.

I would spend time looking at photos of children I knew, considering what was present in their face that 'belonged' to each of their parents. At night I would imagine a baby with features I couldn't recognise. *What if I did not love my baby's face?* I also couldn't quite resolve how to select the race of a donor – in terms of what was important to me the donors in my search results were most often men of colour, but it did not feel right to me that as a white woman I could have a baby who would face discrimination and prejudice I did not suffer. A puritanical voice in me suggested only romantic love should lead to me having a mixed-race child – I should not have the right to choose one given how fetishised mixed-race children can be in white culture. I projected into the future, thinking of all the grievances a child might have against me for bringing them into the world.

This choice, this vital step in the roguish possibility of becoming pregnant, felt insurmountable. I decided to get on with the other steps, believing if I cleared the path, I would be able to make a choice when the time came.

When I saw my GP about the polyp, in the hope of getting a referral, I explained why it was so important to me to have it removed. She told me, 'You need to tell the consultant it is bleeding a lot, otherwise they won't deem it clinically necessary until you try and fail a number of times at pregnancy.' So, I saw a consultant and I told her it bled, and she asked me how I was going to get pregnant and when I told her I was looking at IVF or intrauterine insemination she said 'don't bother, just have a one-night stand.'

During this time, I felt aggrieved that as a single person the state would not help me. My life's desire – my seemingly urgent need to live out the cycle of life as others did – was not approved of, not deemed necessary for a single person. In the criteria listed on the NHS's website, single people aren't even mentioned. You can only access support if you are forty-two or under and have been having unprotected sex for two years or have had twelve failed cycles of artificial insemination. Unprotected sex in this context assumes heterosexual penetrative intercourse, so if you're single or if you're in a queer relationship the NHS is not there for you until you've already sought private treatment that will have run up a bill of tens of thousands of pounds. You are priced out of parenthood, you are confronted with barriers to having a baby that for most people will be insurmountable. In an equal society, wouldn't donor sperm be offered through the NHS?

Under this system, having a baby would only become an option to me should I be rich enough to do it alone, or if I were willing to have sex with someone dishonestly, willing to see them as a means to an end. I found that I could not do that – I don't know how much of it was linked to my fear of rejection, putting myself in a situation where I asked to be desired, where I would have to make myself vulnerable. The mission of having a baby seemed to leave no room for vulnerability. And I didn't feel it was OK to trick someone into parenting, whether they'd end up involved or not. My parents had wanted to have a big family, but over time I felt strongly that my dad resented having children, and by the time I got to double figures, I felt he not only resented parenting but actively disliked me. I wanted my child to respect my choices; choosing and pursuing pregnancy with an unwilling parent felt like a betrayal of the child. I was slowly realising how challenging it would be financially, not just to parent but to attempt pregnancy in the first place and to attempt it responsibly, with intent and with answers to all the tricky *how did I come to be me* questions a future child might ask of me.

I realised I could not afford IVF and would need to have intrauterine insemination instead. I looked at the cost of sperm and saw there was a premium to pay for the most vigorous samples. I could only afford to buy one vial of sperm, and even that would need to be paid for on a credit card. I explored the option of co-parenting, where you are matched with a sperm donor who would require no payment. Some of these men were motivated by a desire to be parents themselves, and wanted a relationship with the child they'd help to make. Others said they were just keen to help someone else's dream come true. I deleted my profile after I received offers of sperm from one too many men who insisted on 'natural insemination' for their donation. A few friends suggested I ask a male friend to donate their sperm to me, but that felt loaded with the possibility of rejection I did not want to experience. Besides, they all knew what I wanted and none of them offered, and nor was it fair for me to expect them to.

On the occasions I allowed the sea fret of my anxiety about how I would get pregnant to lift, I would daydream a little, my daydreams all the tropes of maternal life. A baby at my breast. Milk, vomit, shit. A sleeping toddler with curls stuck to their head and cover thrown off in the night. A tiny hand latched on to my finger. My appearance deranged with lack of sleep. Little dresses and rompers on little hangers. My soft round body, sore, golden, impressive. But also, a sense of incredible companionship, of me arm in arm with a comrade, *it's you and me against the world, kiddo*. I began to feel differently about my abortion. No regret, but a deeply reflective feeling that I might have missed the one chance I had, and a sense of wonder that I could, by this time, have a child about to turn eighteen, a young adult almost the age I was when I became pregnant.

I wondered what I could have learned from that child, how they would have surprised and challenged me, changed me. I saw on Twitter that my old boyfriend, the abortion boyfriend, had had a baby girl. I had to hide him from my feed, afraid to encounter photos of his daughter in case her image became fixed in my mind, a counterfeit of what my own child might have looked like. It can sometimes feel like society isn't keen on airing these thoughts of ambivalence. The way in which I can be a passionate advocate of access to free, safe, legal abortion as well as have complicated feelings about my own experience, sometimes wondering *what if?* In funnelling people into polarised positions, in resisting the difficulty of feeling several things simultaneously, we flatten the texture of life as it is truly experienced. For I can experience the question *do you have kids?* as a painful, awkward question to answer, even if I don't experience the lived reality of *no, I don't* as wholly painful and awkward.

*

My mum came to stay with me so she could be there when I had the polyp removed. These days they do that while you're awake, with no sort of anaesthetic. I was told to take over-the-counter pain medication before the procedure. Feet in stirrups, a camera was inserted into my uterus and the images were screened on a monitor near my head. For the first time I saw into my body, and it reminded me of coral – pink, tender tendrils moving as though underwater. I found I could not look at the monitor when the surgeon began to cut away at the polyp. It hurt, a strange kind of pain, one I'd not felt on the interior of my body before, as though I was being repeatedly stung. Mum held my hand.

Though I thought about my plans all the time, and in some ways I had made a lot of progress, I resisted answering many questions about how I would make it work in practice. My sister repeatedly brought up the impracticality of living in London as a single parent, without her or my mum close by to help. She and my mum encouraged me to investigate childcare costs, how much I'd need to save during maternity leave to support myself. I'd get cross, telling them I could only deal with one big decision at a time. This decision to have a baby felt like it needed to exist in a clearing, guarded by a circle of trees or stones: as though if I let people get too close to it they might contaminate it, or break the spell of my desire – their interest felt a threat. The intrusion of how impossible being a parent might make my life, how hard it would be, how much I'd have to give up to make it work, to make my child's life safe and secure, was too dangerous to consider. The danger being, I might spook myself out of it. Other people I knew, including single parents, told me to do whatever it took to make it happen, not to worry as things would work out. One friend told me how deeply she missed her life before becoming a parent, how hard it was and how painful it was to face her regret, even though she loved her child ceaselessly.

Instead of confronting the challenging realities of seeing my plan through, I occupied myself with the logistics of getting sperm delivered at the right time, working through endless possibilities, and worrying about whether I could create space in the freezer and if the freezer worked well enough to store sperm. It is only now I can see how marvellously I rechannelled my anxieties into spaces that were inconsequential, that gave the appearance of doing something. I turned thirty-eight, then thirty-nine. I don't even know how the time passed, save for how my brain calculated horrible things, like: in a best-case scenario, how many years will I have left with my mum, how long will my child know her, how many good years might a child have with me? I thought about how urgently I needed my mum, how unfair it might be to leave an adult child without a mother. I made lists of baby names. I cried thinking of my friends' children. I cried at friends' pregnancies. In a mental register I noted how almost all the men whom I'd been involved with had children now, and I felt raw with *it's unfair*. These boy-men, who never made their beds, who lived on corner shop chiller-fridge pasties and cereal, who had treated me carelessly. How was it they got to parent, got to look into the eyes of a person they'd made? All kinds of judgement rained down in my mind. I held within me the intent of making it happen for myself, the only antidote to my envy of the complete lives of others, but I held that intent as though intent were enough. All the while my chances of success diminished, shrinking like an apple that's drying out, until all that is left is something you have no choice but to discard. On a trip to Sri Lanka, I bought a newborn-size white lace gown, even though I was gnawed at by a sense this might invite bad luck – *if you buy this, it won't happen.*

I have tried to work out what happened between having the polyp removed when I was thirty-seven (a clearing of the path ahead) and now. I know that the desire I'd felt so intensely in my body and mind became milder and the frenzied need I'd felt was displaced by the burgeoning chaos in my friend Roddy's life, as he became seriously unwell. My mothering instinct redirected wholly, if inconsistently, towards him – encompassing care that was domestic, social, even at times spiritual in seeking faith he would recover. I have not actively abandoned my hope of becoming a mother, but it has gone through dormancy and growth, like poppies that have self-seeded, requiring nothing of me to grow again, bright and surprising each time. Around the time I turned forty, I went to a literary event on motherhood and there seemed to be some conflict between the speakers, or at least I projected one onto them, and I remember feeling so stressed I left during the Q&A. I wrote down one of the things a panel member said, 'It seems so awful to make something live, like what an awful thing to do. Or bold, depending on what you think.' I was still trying to work out what I thought.

I recently found the letter the fertility doctor wrote to my GP about the polyp they'd found during the scan of my uterus. It begins:

> Amy Key came to see me today as she is thinking about having a baby on her own using a sperm donor as she is now thirty-seven and sadly has not met an ideal partner to have children with. We scanned her today and were pleased to note that she has ovaries that contain many follicles, suggesting

that her ovarian reserve is better than average for her age, which is good news.

I read this letter and I began to shake with tears. At the time that mention of the lack of a partner had not hurt me in the way it did on rereading, but there was also pain in realising how close I'd been to a different type of life. There was another document, detailing the results of the scan – fifteen antral follicles were identified in each ovary. Six years had passed; what would my ovarian reserve be like now? I wondered. It made me think of how things decay, suggesting a cucumber in the salad tray of the fridge. How if you forget about it, its insides give way, become a dank mush inside shrink-wrapped plastic. When does the cucumber lose itself and at what point might I have saved it?

Since the rereading, almost daily I hear the letter speak to me, 'sadly' it says, 'sadly'.

*

The nightmare I had about the aborted baby is still in rotation in different guises: sometimes it is a baby (usually *my* baby), sometimes it is the child of a friend. Other times it is one of my nieces or nephews who has been entrusted to my care. Occasionally it is a cat or other small animal of intimidating vulnerability. The fragmented narrative of these dreams usually involves a desperate quest to keep the child or creature alive until I can convey it to safety. I always encounter a threat to that mission, accidentally losing or leaving the 'baby' symbol somewhere mundane but perilous – on a bus, or in a carrier bag, or once outside a nightclub in Newcastle – because of my inadequacies and negligence.

My two cats are predominately house cats. I adore them and want them to be happy, but I have curtailed their freedom, put limits on their pleasure. They come out into my small garden, paws tentative on the unusual, patioed surface. They sniff with suspicion the perimeter where other cats patrol, lie in the sun next to me as I read and drink wine in the summer. But I cannot cope with them escaping the boundaries of the space, I call them back to me if they get close. They are my reminders that I'm not cut out for parenthood. If I can't allow a cat to roam, how would I contend with a child living independently, out of my line of vision, subject to all life's griefs?

If I were a parent, would I be controlling, smotheringly protective, a person my child would have to be liberated from? Might I actively cause them harm? When my cats are unwell, I am gripped by a catastrophic anxiety, which has at its heart: I cannot survive the loss of them. They aren't happy to be picked up, so even getting one of them into a cat carrier can be a day-long mission. How can I parent if I can't even coax a cat into its box? What is the secret of people who can tolerate the anxiety of their cats roaming free through local gardens and streets, being petted and fed by neighbours, colliding with stranger cats in a new territory? What is the secret of people who have mastered the fear of loss enough to take parenting on? How do they sleep? I can't help but feel it is the security, the faith of romantic love, that gives people the resilience and optimism to try.

Each time a friend says they don't plan to have children I feel a deep relief that someone I am close to affirms my child ambivalence and will also live alongside the danger of (if only occasional) regret. Still, I always suspect their minds will change. Each time someone near my age reveals their own desire to become pregnant, or their regret that they did not, my veins are flushed. It's a panic that makes me want to suppress those kinds of conversations, and this panic is detected by people I love, leading to friends worrying over how and when to tell me they are pregnant, leading to friends worrying their joy will upset me. One even wrote me a letter, thinking it would be easier for me to take the news that way. It feels humiliating to be a person who has to be carefully managed, but their caution is not unwarranted.

I sometimes imagine receiving news that someone I know is pregnant in order to test my reaction and feel more prepared, should that news come. It can become ridiculous, and comically unjustifiable, extending even to strangers. I found myself imagining that the writer Sheila Heti had a baby. Even the idea made me feel personally betrayed, because I'd read her book *Motherhood* and found her lack of resolution so comforting. In my mind I'd recruited Heti as a companion of ambivalence, and since she had one of the two things I wanted, romantic love, I thought it unjust that in my fantasy she got to be a mother too. Maybe I was more like those women who called the *Daily Mirror* about teen mums, as I sorted people into categories of who I felt somehow deserved to be a parent and who did not. But inevitably I would turn that question in on myself, and I couldn't muster enough of an argument for why I deserved a baby. There were too many things that could go wrong. I was too afraid.

I want to believe that I can experience mothering and create a family of my own without taking on the status of being a parent, be emboldened by what queer people have done for centuries – find a chosen family. Mothering could be my being important in the life of the children I know. Or I could be someone's 'mother of the heart', the phrase Maggie Nelson borrowed from poet Dana Ward, mothering in ways I did not name as such, but that made another person feel mothered. I might even be mothering now, through practical acts like regularly convening the friendship group to spend time around my dining table or sending a broke friend some money to get them through to pay day. Or in the subtler ways I've contributed to how someone in my life lives, the ways in which we adopt one another's political, social and cultural interests and integrate those in our own. Perhaps I've given them a song that has become part of their canon, cooked for them a dish they recreate time and again, passing on my tastes to others like a gift.

But I don't know how to quieten the scared voice in me that asks if that will be enough, if I will grieve the strange permanence in the world I imagine having a child can give you, one that seems hard to replicate in other ways. I've tried to identify the impulse that drove my desire to have a baby, and I know I briefly felt the biological desire. I felt the cultural desire to a certain extent – for conformity. But overall, I think my desire had vanity at its heart. I wanted through motherhood to give myself another try at existing. I thought it might ease my fear of my own disappearance from the world, of my being an endling. If a child shouldn't be born for that reason, what reason is acceptable? My scared voice also asks if it's truly possible to have a chosen family when, for me at least, almost everyone in it is tied romantically to another, or will be, their sense of family closing in on itself as they couple up and have kids. I feel frustrated with myself for wanting to be someone's number one. To be their person.

My friend Tom dreamed I had a baby girl, texting me to tell me about it, saying I was very happy. In his dream I'd eaten a ham sandwich after the labour and had a bit of ham stuck to my lip. 'Sounds like me, lol,' I replied by text, trying to keep it light. It seemed obvious to me that I'd be ravenous after labour. I thought of the Studio Ghibli animation *Ponyo*, and Ponyo's delight in eating ham for the first time. *Ham!* I exclaimed in my mind, the baby of the dream morphing into Ponyo. I envied his dream, or rather, the me inside his dream. I was feeling so sad at the time, I now forget why, but I thought it unfair he'd seen me happy when I hadn't felt that fleeting sensation – *ah! I feel happy* – landing on me in months. Then it occurred to me, a new thought: you lost your nerve. I could not cope with the anxiety of care for and the certainty of harm to a child. To my child. Another new thought occurs now: I can live without a baby but not without romantic love. In that way a kind of choice has been made, since not deciding is a choice too.

Prior to moving flats, a couple of years back, I slowly went through every box, cupboard and drawer making decisions about what to keep, what to give away and what to dispose of. I found my positive pregnancy test from 1998. I'd consciously held on to it as though to prove to myself I was capable. It had become a dingy emblem of loss. It had survived the cut many times, but on this occasion, I had to let go.

*

When I'm with parents – my friends or colleagues, or perhaps a stranger who is talking about their children as a way of making conversation – I find myself scanning my life for parallels that allow me to join in, to somehow present myself as having parental-type attributes and concerns. This feels important, a way of saying *I too am an adult, my life is as serious as yours*. A strategy I deploy to try to make me feel less annexed from the normative life of a woman my age. I lean heavily on being an aunt, of course, taking on conspiratorial whispers about difficulties with food, sleep, tantrums, or telling stories of how my nieces and nephews came to be given their names. But it doesn't feel good – it's a kind of appropriation that isn't an accurate representation of my relationship with them: those difficulties and decisions aren't mine to speak of. It's an inauthentic accounting for myself. And I wonder who it is I'm trying to coddle or satisfy in playing this part. I recently read something about 'my' category of person: 'Professional Aunt No Kids', or 'PANKs'. I do want to be seen in culture, but I recoil from this type of demographic herding, useful only to marketeers, the qualifier 'professional' giving it away. As if you can only find yourself defined in culture if it's possible to profit from you. Equally I find myself full of shame if I instead lean towards the trope of the *childfree*, with its perky *oh I love kids but it's so great to hand them back to their parents!!!* Because I'm not sure that's how I feel. But it occurs to me I could just contribute to the conversation with questions, with empathetic nods, with genuine interest, rather than seeing those conversations as ones I can't participate in without a story of my own, rather than feeling the rumble of insecurity, the voice that tells me I am just not one of them, I am lesser. If I were just to be myself, the more honest parallel to raising kids is caring for my cats, but who would want to invite the ridicule or pity that can conjure? The cats' presence in my life, their routines – Bambam nudging me awake at 5 a.m. because she wants to be fed, Minnie staring me down at 4 p.m. because that's treat time, Bambam jumping down from her perch when I lie down on my bed, whatever time of day it is, Minnie saying hello each morning with a full body roll – has given me a structure, placed an expectation on me that I welcome. I keep them alive, and they help me live. Perhaps we are mothering each other, perhaps this is the sustained intimacy I wanted and all it takes is my recognition of this to affirm my self-worth.

On the question of why I've not had a baby, of *did you want a baby?* I long for a better, clearer, less cowardly answer. I occasionally try some out: *I can't afford it.* (I couldn't, but that would not have stopped me – logic would not have stopped me but telling someone you can't afford something is a good way to shut down a conversation.) *I can't bring a child into the world because of the climate crisis.* (I'm not that noble.) *I like my life as it is.* (This isn't quite true either.) Then I say to myself *I'm afraid, I'm afraid, I'm afraid.* And in admitting how afraid I was, am, that I am not equal to the task of parenting and that I could not endure the physiological and psychological cost of seeing my child live, whenever I hear someone else's reasons, I think: *you're lying, you're scared too.* How come no one else lets fear be the reason? How is it that some people can stop thinking and just do? Was I wrong to think so hard?

I know you don't avoid risks just by not taking them, avoidance has its own aftermath. In 'Little Green' Joni tells her child that 'sometimes there'll be sorrow' in her life. Joni knows that because she has felt it, is feeling it, will feel it. She made a calculation that the sorrow of living would be less for her child if Joni was not the one to raise her. It didn't mean that the sorrow would be less for Joni herself, or that sorrow could be avoided. If you do, or if you don't, sorrow will attend you.

*

I am now forty-three and my menstrual cycle is again the source of fascination and fear it was when I was a pre-teen. An unusually heavy period, a shortening or lengthening of my cycle, the calcification or escalation of emotional symptoms – all are noted grimly. I google 'perimenopause' with increasing regularity, but I am afraid to consider the results too deeply. I read and reread an essay by the poet Mary Ruefle where she warns you cannot prepare for it, that menopause will make you feel that 'a kind of wild forest blood runs in your veins'. Sometimes it is a comfort to know that if nothing can be done, you can only do nothing.

But still, I have to confront the fact that I have been clinging to a scrap of magical thought: despite having no partner and despite my lack of attempts to secure one, despite the fact that I've taken no further action to become pregnant alone, I've continued to nurture the hope – or perhaps more accurately, the assumption – that it will just happen. Now I can see clearly ahead to the time when that chance will have vanished.

It seems unlikely that I will discover whether – for me – the rewards of parenthood might compensate enough for its anxieties. I will never know what I could have survived, and that, for now at least, is a relief. Instead, I wait for menopause, the long journey that I'm likely already on, wondering if I will wake one day, like Ruefle did, wanting to fuck 'a tree, or a dog, whichever is closest'.

Roddy once wrote a poem for me called 'The Tao of Amy Key'. Two lines seem especially charged now: 'She has one child, which is her cherished self. / She moves in partial peace across grassland.' When the feeling of loss and the anticipation of regret intrudes, I repeat to myself: not having a baby does not equate to a lack of faith in my own future, or my own ongoingness in the world. It is not emblematic of a pokey life, too filled up with myself.

Instead, I notice how my cherished self is feeling, how expansively my feeling roams. It's far beyond me.

FLOWERS

clean white linen and my fancy French cologne

The rhetoric that you must love yourself before you can expect anyone else to love you can feel like a terrible burden. I know I've felt in a double bind: one of self-loathing, as culture tells me I will not be loved until that is overcome, and then one of dispossession, because I've listened to too many songs that tell me I am no one until somebody loves me. In that framework – the war between self-love as realisation and being loved as self-realisation – I lose on both sides. While self-care – in a superficial sense – can come easy, self-love can feel as remote a possibility as romantic love. If romantic love isn't a key that will unlock my esteem, and self-love feels threatening in its difficulty, I still need to find a shape for my life. Not just for my daily routines of care, but for what I'd like to see, feel and experience in my future.

Joni's songs never tell me I'm nobody because I don't have romantic love. I'm grateful. She doesn't preach that it's only love that will make you. I find comfort in her own uncertainty about what move to make. To stay or leave, whether to dwell on what love takes from us or its gifts. When she sings a song to her lover Carey, love doesn't even come into it. 'Carey' has a jaunty, scrappy quality, as though Joni's a bar-room singer, who casually livens up a weekday session, and the bar's patrons spontaneously chip in on the backing vocals. Sometimes I imagine the recording session for it, and think were the track to run on, I'd hear Joni and her band breaking out into laughter at the end. But its cheerfulness conceals a mild anxiety. Joni's foregone the neat structures she has in place to keep her life together, strayed from her path. Even though she likes 'mean old' Carey who is keeping her in Matala, Crete, she's dreaming of an escape back to her life. Not one of cosy, officiated coupledom (she was in Crete between love affairs, Carey a smile-inducing diversion), but one where her fingernails are clean, and she sleeps in crisp white linens with flowers placed around her room.

I need these things too. They are signs I am taking care. Perhaps that's what Roddy saw in me, in his idea of me as my own child, a 'cherished self'. He sometimes rolled his eyes if I didn't want to go out because I had to work the next day, or when I said I wasn't going to go to the pub after poetry class so I could have a night off drinking. Perhaps he interpreted that as self-love, this parenting of myself. More likely he thought I was being boring – I got the impression that he felt if you were single, and had no domestic commitments, you had no boundaries for living! But I felt that if I could provide for myself a baseline of care, there would eventually be the structural integrity required for my self-love to take flight. Even if going to bed early and having nights off drinking were unequal to all the other things I did that made my life harder, that brought about feelings of shame and self-disgust. Spending more money than I had. Borrowing more money than I could pay back. Posting wincingly candid updates on every tremor of my mood on Facebook and Twitter.

*

When I began to write this book, my friend RMJ suggested I read Susan Sontag's 1983 commencement address to Wellesley College. We'd been chatting about writing; how vulnerable it felt to name feelings and ideas and commit them to a page. She told me Sontag's speech had been helpful for her, with its invocation to 'Be bold!' I looked it up straight away but found myself drawn to another message. Sontag wrote about the symbolism of moving from one place to another, from an old status to a new one. She encouraged the graduating students to think about the experience as 'a model for how you should try to live. As if you were always graduating, ending, and, simultaneously, always beginning.' That's what transitions in status give us, the chance to take stock. *This is where I was, this is where I am.* And then to think towards an imagined future – *this is where I now go.* It struck me that this type of reflection, this assigning of importance to one's own journey through life, is a kind of love.

Heteronormative romantic love comes with some presumed transitions. Which ones to make and in what order. Find a partner, share a home, create a family. These things are evidence of progressing through life in a dignified, definable and correct way. Many people are shut out of those transitions because the law or the culture won't allow it, equal status is denied to them. Or they are only accepted if they adopt the heteronormative way. Some other people struggle through those transitions – perhaps their partner is reluctant to commit to the formality of marriage, perhaps there are affairs, perhaps they want to have children but can't. Others give the impression of gliding with ease from one to the next. In the absence of romantic love, and the arrangements and official transitions it can impose, there is some figuring out to do about what shape to give life and how to care for and love that life.

I've had very few changes in status, and none of the changes that we are conditioned to pay attention to – the ones where everyone around agrees there should be a big emotional carnival to recognise it. (I should catch myself there – I did get a university degree, but I did badly and felt no sense of achievement or emotional attachment to the experience so I did not go to my graduation. I don't even have the certificate.) I've not transitioned from single to married, married to divorced, or from daughter to mother. This lack of status makes me question myself. It's not just that absence of a scaffold on which to erect my identity as I present it to the world – in a peppy, proud bio – *wife, mother, entrepreneur, friend.* It's how provisional I can sometimes feel, down to how I speak. I grew up in Kent and the North-East, and my south/north vowel sounds are constantly in flux, as though I cannot get a hold of some essence of myself, me-ness slipping out of my hand like a bar of soap in the bath. What is more natural, for me to say 'bath' in my southern tones, the 'a' long, or in my northern ones, the 'a' short and the 'b' an attack? Even I'm not sure. My work colleagues have one by one asked me, 'not being funny but where is your accent from?' They've heard me swerve into the northern corners of my speech, something I do when I'm either drunk, nervous or performing. Is it possible to love who I am when one of my most intimate expressions of me – my voice – is inconsistent, too prone to interference?

I want to fix myself in place. To have a voice that isn't corrupted. A home I live in so long it risks me haunting it. A personal branch of the family tree. And though I've never felt that marriage was something I had to do, something that I was absolutely destined for, I realise I've been mentally holding a space for it. I've submitted to superstition. I am reluctant to wear a ring on my ring finger because I was told it was bad luck, doing so would withhold a partner from me. And I have occasionally thought about my theoretical wedding. Like how when a new friend told me she and her husband walked out of their wedding ceremony to 'Carey', inviting the congregation to sing it together, I thought, *damn I wish I'd thought of that*, as though it was something I could have done myself. Or I've found myself daydreaming about what I'd wear. It was hard not to indulge in the ritual of it when for a decade my year would revolve around the various engagements, hen dos and weddings of friends. Oyster-coloured shantung silk cigarette pants and an A-line tunic, with silver leather platform shoes, a Bardot beehive, black eyeliner and pale pink lipstick. A 1930s movie starlet gown in peach satin, my hair in a chignon, a pillbox hat with a white fishnet veil. A 1970s empire-line dress in antique lace, with a square neck and long sleeves, my hair worn long and loose. A tour through my past sartorial obsessions. I dread to think how much debt I would have got into to get married, to try to perfect myself through this one-day performance.

I had read the Sontag speech with competing senses of defiance and insecurity. In the end, one of them won out. I said to myself, resist this, this sense of a wavering self, incomplete until I attain a universally regarded achievement. I need to be intact within my own situation, fend off the sense of my status as a single, childless person as a temporary, undesirable spell, of my own provisionality as a subject.

Self-love has to include a disregard for how other people might perceive me, and living as though life is in the present, rather than something that will start in earnest once certain thresholds have been passed. I sometimes have to say aloud to myself: you do not agree that life's worth should be measured in this way. Don't give the idea the authority to direct your self-criticism for not measuring up. It feels like a life's work. *Repeat it until you mean it. Say it like a friend would.*

*

Without commitments and responsibilities to a predominant other – a partner, a child – I've found myself wanting to identify what commitments and responsibilities I will choose to hold. To shape a life that has its own rituals, events to assign meaning to and rules to live by. Even if only that I will change my bed sheets once a week. Get eight hours' sleep a night. Make sure my nieces and nephews know I love them. Use up leftovers rather than spend money on takeaways. Hang out with my cats. Remember birthdays, sad anniversaries. Put out sunflower hearts for the birds. If I begin to fail in my personal and domestic routines, I sense something is up, that more disorder could elbow in. These routines are the tenets of my self-care, and gesture towards self-love.

I've never felt sure how to love myself. I am also unsure if I really know how it feels to be loved well romantically. Or at least, my memories of reciprocal romantic love have curdled with age. So I've always felt curious about the ways in which self-care and its attendant promise of self-love manifests for other women. Which one they buy into, or how they've been able to reject the lot of it. Two broad categories suggest themselves to me. The first is the self-love that is affirmation-based, *I am enough I am a strong woman I am beautiful I can do it YOU GO GIRL*. The sort of self-love that can propel a woman to dump a no-good lover, to protect her boundaries, to apply for that job and ask for that raise! The second is the self-love that enables femininity to be performed, ostensibly for the benefit of the self but with the heavy inference it will make you more loveable – skincare routines, workouts, haircuts and colours, deep cleanses, diets and potions. The sort of self-love that promises to triumph over everything about your body that detracts from the radiant, unattainable, or at least unsustainable, image of the best you.

The former category of self-care, to me at least, only feels accessible when there is a challenge to overcome. I've certainly commanded myself to *come on Amy, you can do this*, motoring myself into cleaning the bathroom. Or I've instructed myself to sort out an irritating banality via an acidic little Post-it. I even have a magnetic memo board on my fridge, one you fix peg letters onto, as though displaying a menu or price list. One of the things on mine implores me to DO THE FUCKING THING. The 'thing' in question being writing. But that does not feel possible as a permanent state of mind, or even as a daily practice, and the line between encouragement and critique is thick and gluey, a space of entrapment. The latter category of self-love I play along with to a certain extent. I have all the creams and elixirs and I try to adhere to their directions for use, but the pampering marketplace (the salons, the spas, the therapists) often make me feel ugly and acutely uncomfortable. If I'm honest, there has always been a bigger dopamine hit in tweezing a lone hair from my face – especially the ones that feel sharp, like the quill of a feather escaping from a pillow – than there is getting a professional manicure or a facial or having my hair done.

My hair is one of a small number of features I like about my physical appearance. But now, as greys have begun to intrude in disturbing numbers, I find I need to visit the hairdresser more frequently than before. I hate it. There's something ghoulish about being at the salon. The way your head is isolated from your body by a sweeping black gown. The confrontation with your own face in the mirror for several hours, your mind ticking with *is that really what I look like?* I never feel uglier than when I see myself in a hairdresser's mirror. I also feel uneasy about the peculiar intimacy of the transaction. The scalp massage during a shampoo, the access given to the back of my neck, the hairs on the arm of the hairdresser close to my lips. It's not because I'm prudish, it's more that there is no one in my life who gets those angles on me. I can't help but wonder if the hairdresser finds me disgusting, wants to be away from my skin. Rolls their eyes as they go to mix more colour. I become a small person, apologising for the thickness of my hair, how hard it is to brush through after it's been washed, how long it takes to dry. 'I'm sorry, your arm must be tired,' I say. I feel bad they have to talk to me, my chit-chat has never been especially good. I have no idea how to be or who even is *myself* in these situations. I am playing a role – a person for whom the hair salon is 'me time' – all the while squirming with distress in my plush leather seat. While I am usually relieved by the results of the visit, walking out of the salon slightly bolder than I entered it, wondering if I will be noticed, my ego makes it all an ordeal. It's wasted emotional effort on my part. The hairdresser likely does not give me a moment's thought, I'm just work to them.

If I can't yet truly love myself, and the cost of that is being unworthy of other people's love, what I'm left with is a kind of *fake it until you make it* approach, a pursuit of compassion for the worst feelings I have about myself and an openness to accepting what others see as good in me. I strive – but don't always manage – to be a person who is capable of care, loving attention, support, companionship, and able to direct that to myself as well as others. Part of this is a reaction to men I've known who seemingly evolved into humanity, into feeling their lives were worth attending to, through the act of falling in love. They waited for someone to come along and spur them into being, none more so than my friend Roddy, who at times thought I might be the one to help him do it. I think of how these men transformed themselves from people of austere and stunted emotional health into loving humans, comfortable with both the expression and receipt of love. Every time I do something with the explicit goal of looking after myself beyond my basic needs, I am acting in defiance of this.

My default mode of self-love hasn't fallen into either of the categories I defined earlier. Mine has been to spend money. Through spending I hoped I'd find a way to like myself more. Be more confident. Be someone people wanted to spend time with. This false promise of love got me into debt, made me indulge every *but why shouldn't I* voice in my head, buying things for myself, paying the bills when out with friends, never saying no when I couldn't afford to do something, showboating, until debt became a way of getting through the month for necessities like travelling to work and the weekly food shop. Paying the minimum payment on huge credit balances and then spending back up to the limit. Ever since I was eighteen and was first offered credit and an overdraft, I've amassed heart-thudding debts, the kind that make you dissociate, as though the debt is a fungus growing in the dark that you have no hand in. *How did it get like this?* I'd ask myself, clueless.

Debt became a means of maintaining a veneer of comfort, a pretty life, of keeping up with others. I'm not always excessive in how I've attempted this. I've bought myself supermarket flowers since my early twenties. Bunches of daffodils, tulips, ecstatically sculptural £2 gladioli – like flower versions of icicles – and all types and colours of cheap roses. I stockpile cheap pink grapefruit-scented bubble bath, never scrimping when I pour it under the running water. I buy good salted butter, olive oil, dark chocolate with salted almonds in it. I have ways of positioning these as essential to maintaining my well-being.

I lose days searching online for perfect somethings. A pair of gold hoop earrings – no specific design in mind, just the thrill of knowing them when I see them – the sweet spot between my aesthetics and price point always a little out of kilter. 'Art Nouveau Wall-Hanging Cabinet Antique.' A discreet but effective toilet brush. Attractive coasters that won't stick to the bottom of cups. And my current obsession: Swedish vintage brass candle sconces. This type of spending is pretty harmless, in that most often I'm not spending at all, I'm just indulging in the pleasure of almost spending, of the chase, perhaps in the same way people can derive pleasure from flicking through potential matches on dating apps, sorting them into yeses and noes but never taking it further. Almost spending is almost erotic.

I often plan my holidays and day trips to towns where charity shops dominate the high street. I enter the shop with a manic determination, circling a couple of times in the same way I used to circle nightclubs, in pursuit of a current or new crush. Just the possibility that my eyes might land on something I want raises my heart rate. On a recent charity shopping mission in Burnham-on-Sea – a seaside town with an amazing charity-shop-to-other-shops ratio – I had a good day. I bought a small onyx bedside lamp and a tiny cabbage-leaf-shaped sauce dish. In the last shop I went into I saw in a glass cabinet a silver brooch in the shape of a maple leaf. It wasn't especially attractive to me in an aesthetic sense, but on the brooch in blue enamel were three initials – R C L. They were my friend Roddy's initials. Charity shops can deliver gifts to you that you could never imagine for yourself. I couldn't leave the shop without taking him with me.

But then there are the extravagant purchases I sometimes spend months or sometimes only seconds contemplating, negotiating a contract of justification with myself. That's why I have a pair of Gucci shoes. That's why I have a handmade non-returnable Liberty-print smock dress that I guessed my size for, hidden in a box in my wardrobe as it is several sizes too big. I go through cycles of binge and purge. A big ASOS order, most sent back, the payment and refund a peculiar way of budgeting. A ruthless sale from my archive, garments pulled from under-bed storage bags, cleaned, pressed, photographed and put on eBay. My efficiency pleases me.

Another ruse I've fallen for in the pursuit of self-love is that everyone should have a signature perfume, which suggests, in its sensory expression, the essence of the wearer. I always wanted one of my own, to get to a point where I might miss *my* 'fancy French cologne'. About a decade ago I found it – Portrait of a Lady. I asked for it for Christmas, my family clubbing together to buy it for me. It has become *my* perfume. The marketing blurb for it asks you to 'consider the perfume a portrait of its wearer'. If my friends pass someone else on the street wearing it, they recognise it and I am brought to their mind.

The hit of buying something just for me, something exhilaratingly unnecessary, is so deeply engrained in my behaviour I've rarely been able to control it, and I know it isn't a loving habit. As bell hooks observed, 'We may not have enough love but we can always shop.' I have been addicted to the hovering promise of a fix since my late teens when at a branch of Topshop I was offered a store credit card and could suddenly have more than I could pay for. Of transformation from dissatisfied to satisfied, from dull to glowing. The potential to go from single to coupled up has been too compelling. It still is. Perhaps it was just a matter of getting the spell right – buying the right thing – which would prompt the desired transition. A slot machine I might win big at.

I know that at its worst my shopping has been very harmful. It has limited my ability to make the moves I've wanted to make – if I'd not had over £30k of debt when I took the redundancy payout from the civil service, I would have felt rich with options; instead I felt the relief of being rescued from a fate I considered to be irreparably bleak. At its best the way I've shopped is an expression of my naivety. A belief the love I have for an object will somehow radiate love in reciprocation, or make others love me. I'm always at war with this impulse. My expensive perfume is never a source of regret but plenty of other things are, or if not regret they pose awkward questions. I love my Gucci shoes – they are classic and practical. Black suede, a low block heel, twin G insignia. I congratulate myself for investing in something so wearable, so remote from a passing trend. But on an intellectual level I've duped myself. Sure, the shoes are attractive and solidly made – but they scream an allegiance to a particular type of lifestyle – wealthy and conservative. In wearing them, am I attempting to cosplay that world, a world I can find appalling, wasteful and crass? If I bought the Gucci shoes to help me stand up tall in the world, confident and chic, I also bought them hoping others would see me that way too.

I know there's a relationship between the way I've spent money to try to create an image of myself that might appeal to others, and the times I've desired to be loved by men who were indifferent towards me. To be cured of the want for approval from those who will never give it, those who I have ambivalent feelings about. That seems to be the task I will always work at. To spot when I'm craving a status that I don't believe in. Then there's the Liberty smock dress. My intuition told me the dress would most probably not suit me, but I wanted to buy it anyway, to be a woman who could look dainty in a loose, old-fashioned dress. All clavicles and flatness. Buying the dress was a rejection of my body, which would not fit the image of me in the dress that I had in my head. If the best things in life are free, the best of all is romantic love. How much do I need to spend to fill the gap love's absence has made?

On my good days I am able to strip back to simple things that make me feel cared for, the love that is to do with safety, warmth, stability. The 'clean white linens' Joni longs for in 'Carey', and making my bed each morning. Sharing out a bunch of flowers between four vases – one for the kitchen windowsill, one for my bedside, a stem or two for the toilet, the biggest vase for the coffee table. Changing into my comfy clothes after work and then into fresh pyjamas before bed. Standing in the sun in the garden for a minute or two with my eyes closed, sensing the sunlight within me. Turning off the TV or music to tune in to birdsong when I hear it. Getting an early night. Learning a new song. Chatting to my family. Saying no to an invitation or a demand that will bring stress. Self-care is as much about what you don't do as it is what you do. These are loving actions. Habits that are a daily commitment to myself that can reliably bring about pleasure, or calm, or comfort without the need for another.

I feel as though I'm getting somewhere with those habits, getting somewhere with my overspending, recognising how quickly it undoes all the care I've tried to put in place for myself. But to give life more shape than the succession of days lived well I've also begun to think about what transitions have been important to me, and what transitions I might want to mark in the future.

A few years ago, I commissioned a ring from the jeweller Tessa Metcalfe. *Poetry* magazine had taken two of my poems and I had shrieked with delight. They paid by the line, and it was more money than I'd ever made from my poetry. It was a different kind of spending, less about trying to create an image of myself that others would recognise as accomplished, secure, interesting, and more about giving myself a symbol to bring me back to myself. Tessa's practice is to set jewels in gold castings of pigeon claws. In her creations, it's as though the jewels have been scavenged, stolen by the claws, and in their grasp are presented to the world with a thrilling, near vulgar defiance.

I've always had a thing for opals. When my grandma's aunt died, my grandma gave me and my siblings £10 each from her inheritance. We were to use this to buy an outfit to wear at my grandparents' ruby wedding celebration. I was eight at the time and had recently had my ears pierced. For my outfit I chose red chinos, a red-and-black polka-dotted blouse and a red, double-breasted cardigan. I also chose some earrings – opal studs – to replace the ones that I'd been pierced with. I'm not even sure if they were real or fake. But it seemed fitting that for the ring I had made, I choose opal again, its galactic flashes of fire and polar ice, its inherent vulnerability. And as the opal was faceted, it was even more vulnerable.

'What happens if it breaks?' I asked Tessa. 'We'll deal with that if and when it happens,' she said, 'you just have to love it and wear it.' I wanted to look at life like Tessa, to find its precarity beautiful. But fear for the future of the opal on my finger nibbled away at my pleasure – perhaps it was an act of self-sabotage to incorporate such fragility into my daily routine? It took some time to come to terms with the possibility that it might not last forever.

My decision to have an expensive and impractical ring made for myself had tones of Carrie Bradshaw in *Sex and the City*. In the episode I'm thinking of, 'A Woman's Right to Shoes', Carrie sets up a gift registry at Manolo Blahnik in protest at her married and parenting friends not appreciating how she celebrated and paid out for their exciting changes in status. The similarity made me squirm a little, even though I cheered Carrie on.

When I bought the ring, I wasn't saying *I'm single so I'm marrying myself!* like a vapid banner of feminist empowerment, attainable only by buying into the traditions that had no place for me. Instead I was attempting to mark a change in my status: I was moving across the threshold from my thirties to my forties, and I was about to publish my second collection of poems. I wanted a carnival of my own.

With this action I tried to establish my own tradition of finding a way to mark my life's occasions with something – with an object – that would help me remember and acknowledge transitions of my own: leaving my civil service job after thirteen years (a holiday to Sri Lanka), publishing my first book of poems (a party), having one of my paintings chosen to illustrate a story in a magazine (bought a painting from a friend), paying off my consumer debt (solemnly wrote 'Day One' on my wall calendar). If I didn't note these milestones, they would often go unmarked. Not because the people around me are unkind or thoughtless, but because it's not easy for them to see the importance of these transitions for me. They have no equivalent in life's presumed structure: we're not preprogrammed to assign significance and attention to them in the way we are for births, marriages, anniversaries. I'm not saying I wish the things that have been personally important for me were commodified in the same way as say a wedding might be – with bespoke stationery, colour schemes, venue hire and several celebratory meals that family and friends would be expected to drop everything for. But I do wish the culture I grew up in, and the white, hetero culture I'm funnelled into, was not so unimaginative and hierarchical in its ability to recognise other life transitions that might be worth marking.

Without this openness from others, it takes a person who is willing to make a fuss of their own life to have their occasions noted. Or that noting becomes a private act that no one else can acknowledge, because to celebrate oneself is shameful, greedy, undignified behaviour. What are we missing of our friends' and family members' lives that are every bit as important as a change in legal status or the growth of a family? I fear it's so many things. You might call my practice of noticing and marking things for myself self-love. But I don't want these objects that symbolise so much for me to be symbols only I can recognise. I want the thresholds that I cross over to be celebrated by others too. When this happens it means so much. The symbolism of some vintage forget-me-not-blue glass buttons and a length of hydrangea-blue lace sent to me by my friend Camellia. The significance of a spring bouquet of white tulips and blue hyacinths that

Becky timed to reach me when they would say something very specific.

*

I've recently been reflecting on how I've written poems to be read at weddings, seven of them. I laboured over these poems to create a compression of intimate details of the relationship, saturated with things that hold meaning for the couple but could also be recognised by the guests as a poem of love, recognised as *weddingy*. Of those seven marriages, three are now over. Do I resent the effort of the poems for those three? The hotels, the travel, wedding outfits and gifts? I do not. I don't believe that experiences or commitments lose importance in their demise. But I notice how the transitions we're socialised to celebrate are ones seen as singularities – a commitment for life, the birth of an individual – even though they come with their own entourage of celebrations attached. Engagement cards, hen dos, baby showers, first birthday parties. Each of these transitions is marked over and over. It is expected, and for some people seems to create an annual sore point if the celebration is more muted than they'd like. I wonder how satisfying are these corporate-sized celebrations for the people involved? I've certainly experienced how the loading of import onto a once-in-a-lifetime experience has left my friends full of doubt, guilt, stress and debt, adrift from their original intent. I can't help but think it would be better if, instead of sticking to what is accepted as worth celebrating, we were encouraged to celebrate what is personally meaningful for us.

In thinking about this I've realised that there is something to the affirmation-based self-love category that's worthy of more of my attention. Because when we affirm ourselves, we are borrowing the voice of a friend to help us believe in our worth. To note my own transitions and ask others to celebrate with me I have to start from a position of self-respect and love. If I allow myself to momentarily overlook how self-love is sold to me and my rejection of it on the grounds of how it's co-opted (invented?) to serve capitalism, I realise I need it. Being without romantic love has led me to consider the question *what is wrong with me* with such dailiness, I may as well be asking myself *what's for tea*. I still struggle to dismiss the idea that if only I could love myself, love would follow. Finding someone being the inevitable outcome of the output of my self-love.

In the early years of perpetual singleness, I drew the most simplistic of conclusions: *I should lose weight*. Every diary I've ever kept has a cruel list somewhere in it and on all those lists is 'lose weight'. At first, I was able to simply stop eating and for the first time in my life I became thin. Then, when that didn't stick, I attempted regime after regime. For years I would make myself sick after almost every single meal. Now, as a much fatter person than I was in my twenties and thirties, I realise how sad it was that I thought weight was what stood between me and love. Sad because I was just a lovely young plump woman who was being unkind to her body, and sad because I'd chosen not to see that fat people are loved, are desired and are in romantic relationships – and I could have been too. I thought I should not expect and did not deserve love until I'd resolved the problem of myself. And by lacking confidence, I'd made things even worse – because after all, confidence is attractive and if you can't be thin, you must at the very least be confident if you expect anyone to find you attractive despite your aesthetic failing. A newly fat woman is often described as having *let herself go* as though she didn't love herself enough to stay slim. I think perhaps the opposite is true – a women who grows comfortable enough to be fat might be making peace, learning to accept herself as she is rather than punish herself with restraint. In my heart, I know the times I've *let myself go* have been not to do with how I look, but instead they've been the occasions I've supplanted myself for another's approval. But now as a fat, single woman in my forties I'm aware of the charges society has against me: I'm to blame for my fatness, my singleness is a natural consequence of the fatness and the undesirability of my age is something I should accept as the way it goes for women in heteronormative life. I've scored a hat-trick.

One of the cruelties of femme presentation in the world is how you can never catch your own beauty in the moment. Like the way I can now see, really see, without it being something I might have said in the hope the saying could make it so, how all young women are beautiful, how the youth in young women is so impossibly lovely. When you're in your twenties and a woman in her forties says, *you don't know how lovely you are*, you shake your head. Then you're thirty and a woman in her fifties says it, then you're forty and a woman in her sixties says it. And so it goes on. *You're so young!* is a refrain you will hear in every decade of your life. But each time you will shake your head and think, *no*, even though it's you who now finds yourself saying this to younger women. At every interval you'll deny your own loveliness. You'll be seventy years old with chic silver hair cut into a bob, a face full of interest like the weave of an extraordinary silk, and a young woman will say *I hope I look like you when I'm older*. No, you'll think. No.

What might have been different in my life if I'd said to myself back then *I am beautiful, I am enough* and learned to mean it? What might have been different if my mum wasn't constantly shamed into dieting, making 'womanness' seem to me like a project of constant aesthetic vigilance? If one of the only letters my dad has ever written to me didn't open by saying 'love, you must really do some exercise.' Or if I had disregarded the notion of being beautiful altogether and instead valued other possibilities of life – friendship, creativity, community? Being kind to oneself, loving yourself, seems to take a concerted effort. Yet it is prescribed not as a complete goal in itself, but one that will lead to easier attainment of romantic love (*if you're happy and content, love will come to you!*), or easier decision-making about love that does not serve you (*I deserve more than this person offers*).

Recently I've tried to look at photos of myself with the eyes of someone who loves me, to be a friend to myself. Because who among our friends do we not love to look at? It always surprises me that a friend will take a photo of me and say 'I love this photo of you,' or 'you look great in this photo,' and I'll be alarmed. It fucks with my self-image, which always seems to lag a few years behind the reality of my current one: *they think this looks good, this is how they see me*, I think with incredulity, insulted. But now I try to say to them 'post whichever photo you like' more than I say 'please delete that one'. I can't manage to look at myself and think, *you are beautiful*, but I have begun to be able to think more compassionately: *this is your body. This is your one body.* And sometimes, *you look happy, you are laughing*.

'I just want you to be happy' is something we hear from the people who love us. 'All that matters is that you're happy.' The question of *what makes you happy* seems to float in the public consciousness – a quiz, a magazine article, a dating app prompt. I am never quite sure what my answer is. Happiness is something that I cannot always summon, it's more like a butterfly landing on me briefly. *You're in the world*, it seems to say to me, a moment of connection that is impossible to manufacture. But there have been some things in my life that have been dependable in their ability to generate a kind of happy-adjacent feeling. Not *the butterfly has landed on me* feeling, but *a possibility of a butterfly landing on me* feeling.

*

One of my most precious possessions is a small, falling-apart notebook. Many of the historical documents of my family were destroyed by my paternal grandfather before his death from bowel cancer. This notebook has remained almost intact (save for some pages cut out of it – who knows by whom). It is a diary, begun by his aunt, Mabel Evelyn Key, in 1926. There are poems and mottos she has copied out, self-portraits in silhouette, drawings of pigs with the rascally comment alongside of 'Bacon of the future!' But it is mainly a document of hardship and sorrow, opening with the recording of 'Mother died, Dec. 3rd 1919. Bro Bob lost at sea Oct. 29th 1916'. Mabel had the responsibility of 'keeping house' from the age of fifteen and lots of what she wrote about was doing without. Her life, and her wants – just to be wished a happy birthday when 'not a soul remembered', to be thanked for her labour in the home, to be able to fill a stocking for her 'only pal', her brother John who died by drowning just before Christmas – throw my own excessiveness into sharp contrast. This diary is something I turn to when I am wallowing in my own lack, when I am losing perspective on what I need. Mabel's needs were so paltry, she was so let down. I have boundless riches in comparison. Friends who want to spend my birthday with me. Appreciation from others when I help them.

One intriguing entry for me relates to something Mabel got. In red ink she wrote

> If things proceed as I expect, I am going to see about a bicycle in Sept., then heigh-ho! for the open road. I never get past my own nose, & I am sick of Shields & its sooty streets, & train rides are out of the question, – too expensive. Just wait till I get a bike, I'll show them!

On the pages that follow there are drawings of the bike alongside text that says 'strong as a horse!' and 'all my own work'. The pleasure of it is so vivid. Might I get past 'my own nose' of internet shopping, with its interminable basket-filling and abandonment of things that won't fulfil me? Might I stop acquiring things as though self-love could be achieved through an incremental patching of the material holes I spot in my life?

But underneath the original entry, Mabel added in pencil 'you got your bike, but you also got a lot of things you didn't bargain for – serves you right!' I feel so sad that the bike became a totem of pain for Mabel, who just wanted to ride a bike and have some freedom. I wonder how the bike came to be to blame, if she'd wanted it too much and felt rightly punished for her wants. But maybe it was just her realisation that the longed-for bike did not have the power to displace all that made her unhappy, and all the things I spend my money on cannot do that for me either.

I am still frightened that should my desire for romantic love be fulfilled, another desire will rush in to occupy the space it once took up in my canyon of want. That strange grasping place that assumes what I want will be denied and fixates on improbable solutions. I have watched with distaste how coupled people transfer the need for the house to the need for a wedding, to the need for a child, to the need for a bigger house. The never-ending escalation of desires. How might I resist always wanting – scanning the future for the next unbearable absence that I must resolve, giving in to the emotional occupation of wanting instead of valuing what is? I've come to realise that self-love, for me, requires a rejection of desires that have a material form and a rejection of new statuses and life transitions as a fix for all that feels incomplete. If self-love is about reaching a state of appreciation for myself that grows from actions I take to care for my needs, rather than wants, I am trying to attune to what those needs are. What would quieten the growling feeling of desires that the world of things cannot touch? I wonder if I'd find my greater need is self-friendship. Less intimidating than self-love; warmer. The ordinary joy of supermarket flowers around my room, rather than the unattainable perfection of a long-stemmed, red rose.

BLUE

you know I've been to sea before

'Blue' is the last track on the A-side of the album. It is a complete tonal shift, just Joni and her piano. It feels like *Blue*'s most private song, the intimate heart around which the rest of the songs spin. Joni plays the piano as though she's working out a sketch for a song, hidden from the gaze and ears of others, unselfconscious. It is one of the first pieces of music that I felt I might be able to play myself on the piano. It's only recently that I've tried to.

Joni addresses her lover, 'Hey Blue, there is a song for you.' He is unreachable, far out at sea and caught in the crushing wave-power of addiction. The song is a plea from closer to the shore. She doesn't know if he will even hear it, whether she can get through to him. She wants to know where she stands with him – does he want her anchored alongside him or is she free to sail away? So she leaves the song for him in a shell he can put to his ear when he decides to return. A protected space of mutual intimacy he can enter when he is ready, the song forever calling out. I wonder if for Joni the sea is an overwhelming place, directionless and turbulent. Perhaps Joni prefers rivers, their flow.

From the first listen, I misheard a line in the song as 'song's all I turn to', rather than 'songs are like tattoos'. I liked the way I misheard it. I positioned songs I loved in the feeling part of me, the secret diary part, a place I could turn to for intimate companionship in my emotional experience. I had secrets to keep from an early age. I like the true lyric too; for decades *Blue*'s songs have felt imprinted on me like an invisible code, waiting for romantic love to activate them, for me to find that one person I'd been singing them to all my life. *Blue* became part of my language of intimacy, an intimacy of disclosure, vulnerability, unadorned feeling that I thought I'd eventually share with a romantic other. The radiator warmth of love exposing the words of a letter written in lemon juice, words that say, 'I love you.' A voice only I can hear when I pick up a shell on the shore. A tattoo in a hidden place. Romantic love, the beautiful and inviolable vulnerability of it as expressed in this song, at the centre of experience. All other loves subordinate to it. Of all that romantic love offers that I can feel denied to me, it is intimacy I long for most.

*

'Blue' is the album's fifth track. In the Taylor Swift fandom there is the legend of track five. Swift's fans consider the fifth track on each of her albums to be a kind of link between her and them – a revelatory, personal song. One that speaks to them directly. I'm sure Joni's track order was settled on for other reasons, but the fact that 'Blue' is track five lends it some deeper resonance for me, I allow myself this borrowed additional significance. In the year I was born my family were living in Deal, Kent. Our house was one street back from the seafront. I know it's personal myth-making, something a little too self-involved, but I've always thought that the sea was elemental in the creation of my selfhood. I think of waves as a sound I tuned in to and drew comfort from in my first moments as I might the voice of a parent. I think of how the first air in my lungs was sea air – its mineral lucidity and its mood-sharpening stinks, and of how the earliest skies I knew were a drama of obliterating coastal light, yellow-plastic sunshine, mists and gloom. Even now, to be by the sea is to be in my senses in a way that doesn't seem possible elsewhere. When you're in your senses, you clear a space for truth. The wily part of you is no match for the sea; the sea cannot be deceived, and in the water, I cannot deceive myself either. I am vulnerable and in a state of receiving, ready to listen and ready to speak. It is a kind of intimacy.

So when Joni sings 'you know I've been to sea before', I feel a sincere affinity, a kinship. We both know the feeling of being at sea, uncertain and desperate for an anchor. But we also know how making our way through waves can have a clarifying, therapeutic influence. I let myself think and feel things in water that I resist at all other times. There have been times I've swum out and let my tears slide into the sea. I imagine the sea translating what the tears are speaking of, holding me knowingly, letting pain dissipate into the salt water and lose its potency. I become porous and the sea acts through me, in the way romantic love can make you feel as though you're bleeding through your edges into another person. This evaporation of my own borders, slipping out of myself and into another medium, paradoxically can feel like I am more in my body than ever. If in being romantically alone I lack an attentive witness to my internal life, I sense the sea as one. Even if it will never speak back, my ears are open to what it might say to me.

When I was on the trip to California in February 2020, I was due to travel from Los Angeles to San Antonio to attend a writers' conference for a few days. I would be there with my friend Alyssa, stopping in Austin on the way, then we'd meet my friend from London, Jane, in San Antonio. In the days running up to the conference we were in touch trying to work out whether to stick to our plans given the emergence of Covid-19. Initially, I was quite relaxed. I wrote to Alyssa, 'I'm just taking precautions washing my hands etc.' and felt secure in the fact I'd brought a thermometer with me so I could monitor any symptoms. But with each hour, the news from across the world about how the virus was spreading rapidly gave a more substantial form for my anxiety to grow around. With a day to go, we all decided to cancel the trip to San Antonio. But that left me with other decisions to make. I was supposed to be in the US for another two weeks and suddenly found myself without accommodation for the week ahead. By chance my friend Sophie was in Berkeley on an artists' residency, and perhaps impulsively she invited me to stay with her. One thing I'd been told to do in California – but hadn't included in my initial plans – was to get the Coast Starlight train. This route follows a path along the Californian coastline, as though the train is pulling through a stitch on the coastline's hem. After talking it through with my friends back at home, I bought a business-class ticket for $98, departing the following day.

I decided to spend my last day in LA making a pilgrimage to Joni's old house in Laurel Canyon, where she lived when writing *Blue*. I got a taxi from Silver Lake – a long, straight ride down Sunset Boulevard and up into the hills. We missed the house, so I was dropped some way up the road. Walking down Lookout Mountain Avenue, there were purple flashes of violets, flowering rosemary and thyme. Every green thing had a bleed of blue. I had a difficult feeling in my chest and throat, a tension, as though a rigid flower were attempting to open its petals in me, and I needed to give myself over to it. I stopped for a few minutes and watched young deer spring across the hillside opposite. I picked a violet and closed my hand over it. I was aware of my dramatising of this journey as it happened.

I reached Joni's house and stood on the driveway outside, unsure of what to do. I didn't know if this mission was something other people undertook; it wasn't as though Joni lived there anymore. On my tiptoes I looked over the sage-green fence, and a golden dog appeared in a window on the second floor of the house. It noticed me and began to bark.

Absence of romantic love in my life had created its own awkward space in me. Like a corner of a room you cannot find a comfortable use for, a deficient space grasping for its own utility. And I sense other people can see this and that it makes them uncomfortable. They seek to solve it ('get on the dating apps!') or to refute romance as goal ('I wish I had your freedom'), and some people, the coupled ones who rarely use 'I', all their tastes, habits, opinions tethered to 'we', seem to panic about how to interact with me, like the barking dog sounding the alarm to its owner.

I was uncomfortable too. I didn't understand how I'd got to this place in my life. After standing outside the house for some minutes, taking photos and a video of the deer on the hillside, I picked up a tiny windfall orange and a viola growing from a bank nearby. Then slowly, I walked down the hillside hoping no one would pass by and see me crying. Later that day, I began to write in the notebook I'd been carrying since I left London.

The train journey from Los Angeles to Oakland took a little over ten hours. I told myself I would use that time to work on an essay about how Joni Mitchell's music informed my poetics, which I had pitched to the magazine *Granta*. As the train followed the west coast, I felt my body rearrange itself, and all of who I was reorient towards the blue of the Pacific. I thought of 'Blue', and it began to play in my mind's ear.

It's an easy song to conjure. The piano part is a melody repeatedly rising and falling back on itself, like waves. Joni sketching out the song. Her voice sails on top of the piano. At times her vocal is strong and emphatic – the forward motion of a wave. At others it sounds insecure, strained, as though she has paid out every ounce of her vulnerability and can now only retreat. The song no longer at sail. I'd been putting off listening to the album. I was scared I might not be up to the task of writing about *Blue*, as though Joni's music could only pour into me at a specific angle, and then her voice might pour out of my writing, blended with my own. I opened my laptop, hoping the mere action could pull me into words, but the sea beyond the window was too compelling. I sat twisted towards it, drinking white wine from a plastic cup, imagining I was running at the very edge of the waves, in a gallop that forced my heart up into my throat.

Instead of listening to Joni, risking getting something wrong in how I heard her, I put Joanna Newsom on, beginning with her song 'In California', a kind of proxy for Joni's *Blue* and its Californian anchor. Newsom sings that she's not afraid of anything other than life. I caught myself remembering something I'd read earlier that day. Dipping in and out of phone reception I finally found it on Twitter. It was from Deborah Levy's memoir *The Cost of Living*:

> I stopped by the fountain, only to find it had been switched off. A sign from the council read, 'This fountain has been winterised.' I reckoned that is what had happened to me, too. To live without love is a waste of time.

Joni knew about being winterised. One of the first of her songs that I loved was 'The Gallery' from her album *Clouds*. In it she sings of how her partner had possessed her pretty years, but when their love began to fail, and presumably her prettiness faded, he left her to face winter, to grow old, alone. I hadn't realised I'd winterised myself. I hadn't realised I'd wasted so much time. I've been saving love for a special occasion, like a bottle of wine I'd hung on to, even though it would not age well. I'd given my pretty years to no one. The truth of it coursed through me like a medication administered directly into my blood.

The proximity to the sea had done its emotional work on me, carried me into an intimate state where I could see things as they were, rather than as I might pretend them to be. I bought another half-bottle of wine, drinking to try to numb the grief I felt for myself and to burrow into that grief, deep enough to stand in it. The shore that the train had clung to disappeared then, and after the obscuring hills – which I resented – we passed through oil fields, crops, the scrub, until the sun went down, and I felt dehydrated and bereft. The blue of the sea replaced by the blue of night.

I'd thought my trip to LA would serve two purposes. The primary one was the time to write and think – I'd been awarded a grant to develop my 'creative practice' and it was funding my travel to California and the writing conference in San Antonio. I wanted to step across the threshold from poetry to prose. See what I might find in myself there. This felt brave, for me. I'd always felt unqualified to write or to be taken seriously as a writer. In my mind people who wrote essays and reviews had degrees in literature, MAs in creative writing and inevitably a PhD in something or other. Poetry felt more inclusive, but perhaps that was because of the luck of finding Roddy as a teacher when I was twenty-seven. He wasn't in thrall to academia, didn't seem to lean one way or another in his tastes. And while poetry can be a place of cliquedoms and tedious infights, and people can experience shameful gatekeeping, I felt liberated by a sense of belonging that Roddy helped create. I was accepted as 'a poet' without qualification. I liked that once I met him I suddenly knew lots of other poets, none of them alike, and within Roddy's groups, at least, I needed no entry ticket to be one of them. Still, I wanted to write prose too and I'd found the courage to try. The second purpose of the trip I couldn't have planned for. Roddy had died the previous month and I hoped the trip might also give me a space to grieve him, away from the distraction of work and the containment of my routines.

On the train I went searching for that grief, I thought to myself, *step into it*. But when I stepped into the part of myself that I thought was aching with vulnerability, needing my attention, it was not Roddy I found. Instead, it was a grief that the emotional occupation of Roddy's illness had cleverly hidden.

I realised that I had stopped looking for, and even being open to, romantic love and the things that go alongside it. I'd been seeing myself and the way I was living as making do, a temporary situation. I was waiting, passively, for romantic love to arrive and assign more grandeur to my material and social conditions. A major part of what I considered out of my reach was the physical and emotional intimacy that develops when people are willing to be vulnerable. For me, it felt like romantic love was a precondition of intimacy. Without it, I must cast about for what I can crown as intimate interactions and relationships. Later, I admitted to myself that I sometimes feel a kind of gratitude for my cat's little hot tongue on my hand, when she occasionally includes me in her grooming. I notice what it activates in my body – a feeling of being tended to, like someone briefly stroking my hair. I know the action of my cat is not unnatural, but I worry my experience of it is. The brief pleasure of my cat's attempt to care for me is sharply replaced by shame. How is it that I lack physical intimacy to such a degree that this interaction is a ghostlet of bodily affection? I always thought physical intimacy and sex would be available to me, especially as, for much of my adult life, when I was having sex, I tricked myself into thinking it was romance.

I know sex isn't analogous with intimacy – and sex doesn't require intimacy to be hot. So more than sex, I crave physical and emotional closeness, the intimacy that comes through trust, honest reckonings, love that sees you at your most flinty or gruesome times and accepts you. I crave the erotic potential of physical closeness, a proximity to sex, not a guarantee of it. I crave someone letting themselves go enough to sleep on my shoulder. I crave letting myself do the same. That feeling of being trusted. Then I remember, the sea is sometimes the shoulder I feel able to sleep on. I remember, I've always wanted to fuck in the sea. Friends who have tell me it's not all that, but I still fantasise about it. If the sea is a site of intimacy, the idea of sex in the sea seems to hold within it an even deeper intimacy that I've yet to experience. I'm prepared to be disappointed.

In my mid-twenties my friend Adam invited me to join him and some other friends at his mum's and her partner's house in the South of France. It was my first group holiday abroad. We took turns preparing meals that were both simple and elaborate, slept in, spent all day outdoors, drank late into the night. Each day after breakfast we would pack up a picnic and head to a body of water. There was one within walking distance of the house, a couple of kilometres along the river, which ran behind the village and up into the hills. To get to the plunge pools you'd pick your way back and forth across the river, relying on particular rocks to secure your passage. Eventually you'd reach a small, deep pool, flanked on either side by broad flat rocks where you could arrange yourself with towels and books and sunglasses and beers. The pool was dramatically cold and not everyone would want to get in, but I noticed the older women in the group always did.

One day Adam's mum Judith and her partner Bea went into the water first. I sat at the edge, taking comfort from watching them. They were Marxist, feminist, lesbian, writers. They spoke to me – to all of us younger people – as equals, sought challenge from us, enjoyed the play and rigour of debate. I'm not sure I'd ever experienced that before, had adults deeply interested in what I thought, what I cared about, what scared and excited me. Nothing shouted down. Nor were doors slammed. Those five days in France I felt my brain itching in ways it hadn't since I was a teen, I felt myself wanting to act on something I'd suppressed – a desire to write. I aspired to their easy ways with their bodies, their rejection of patriarchy, their ability to get into the water without hesitation. I wanted to move in this world of confident, secure adults. After a beer, with the pool empty, everyone content in their own time, I slipped into the pool from the edge, screaming with shock. I didn't know how to float then, and so I reached for a pool noodle and clung to it, gently bobbing in the water. For a few moments I cast the noodle away and floated, then panicked a little and grabbed it again. The next day, we went to the seaside. I'd not swum in the Mediterranean before. I wasn't prepared for its fantastic effect – I barely needed to move to stay afloat, and tentatively I turned onto my back, let my neck go. I shimmied my hands a little, imagining my fingers dragging fine strands of light through the water. I felt peace. But there was also a feeling I'd not had before, one of sovereignty over my body. Lying on my back, supported by the salinity, my ears flooded with water. This brought on a sense of complete interiority – a new state in which to encounter the world absolutely in my body. I came to trust not the sea itself, but myself in the sea – it became a place I could anchor myself, reject the notion I needed someone else to do it for me, reject the idea of being crowned by anyone other than me. If I listened to my body, I'd know when the water was safe to enter. I'd understand how to take pleasure in it and how to leave it when my instinct told me it was time.

A fear I often return to is whether intimacy of the self counts. Does self-knowledge have to rebound from another, be in collaboration with someone, to give you the best look at yourself? Otherwise, might I only be hearing myself as echoes? I'm afraid that if I am not seen, heard and observed in the smallest, pettiest, most inconsequential moments of my life, my most basic nature might always be slightly concealed from me. As though my one true self is being withheld by the lack of romantic love. If I try to locate that nature myself, what comes to mind is someone whose ego can be hurt by returning home from a trip to find only junk mail has arrived in their absence. Occasionally I try to catch myself in the act of being me, listen back to the snores, coughs and murmurs captured on my sleep app. I find this self-surveillance creepy, can only bear it for a few seconds, but I do it because I am desperate for feedback. Desperate to know what it is I need to change about myself. I'm afraid that it was my fault I was alone when I heard the worst news of my life; that when I received the most joyous news in my life, again, I was alone. I'm afraid these things tell me that I have done my life wrong. I'm afraid I might not ever truly know myself. Then these thoughts clam up. I'm unable to face them and I hate myself for the indulgence. I know that if you ask yourself hard questions, you must be prepared not to find an answer. You must be prepared to admit sometimes your questions rise from self-pity, helplessness, envy.

*

The emotions I feel while in water – the bath, a lake, the sea, but especially the sea – feel intact and dignified. It's as though water, its vastness and boundary-obliterating quality, strips away any complaint or internal struggle I have in facing up to my feelings and owning them. I am liberated from the self-censure I can feel in conversation with another person, from the fear I might present my emotional content to others in a garish way, or worse, underplay it to the extent my feelings could be heard as miniature and easily disposed of. In Brighton for a friend's hen do, I was aware of some emotional discomforts that threatened to seep out of me, bringing a serrated edge to my tone and expressions. I wanted my friend to have a lovely time, to feel wrapped up in a collective happiness for her forthcoming wedding, but my ugly emotions felt combustible. I was the outlier of the group – the only single woman. The maiden aunt, reaching again for stories about other people's partners, other people's children to join in with the conversation. I'd bought new clothes for the trip, a T-shirt and jeans that were at a slant to my ordinary clothes, things more like my friend's style than my own. I felt foolish. I was faking it. The first night I reached for more drinks to dampen my brittle, flammable feelings. The next morning I reached for the sea.

I walked a few streets away to the beach. I stopped a few metres from the tideline, stripped down to my swimming costume and walked into the sea without hesitating. One by one, everything I felt about myself came into focus in my mind, brightly illuminated. *Come at me*, I thought, as though I needed to take each one down like an arcade game boss. But as I floated, my desire to fight the feelings mellowed. *OK*, I thought. *It's OK*. Back at the house we were staying in, I had a shower and got dressed. I liked the way the jeans looked on me.

When I speak of painful feelings with another person, I am all too often held back by my own censure. That I am being melodramatic. That what I am saying is not what I really mean. That I am boring. I don't have a talent for storytelling out loud, I truncate events to the point of losing narrative grip. My tone belies how I feel. I briskly attempt to redirect any curiosity of the person I am speaking to back towards them. For me, it has felt easier to be the receiver of the story, to listen to, to hold space for the pain of others. I wonder if this has been in part a defence mechanism, a way to feel I am experiencing intimacy without offering my own vulnerability. I wasn't always like this. I cried a lot as a kid – always ready to be moved by something. My siblings teased me for always 'crying to the music' on TV, and my dad undermined any display of emotion as me being 'a prima donna'. So after a while I tried to button myself up, a strategy that often failed, my vulnerabilities seeking their escape in an unanchored state of drunkenness where I'd cry looking at myself in the window of a night bus home, or in the back of a taxi. Cry on the toilet. Cry as I removed my clothes and put on my pyjamas. Cry on social media, flinging my tears online under the cover of ironic public ennui.

A few years back I got norovirus. I'd been to a friend's book launch the night before, drunk a lot and eaten very little. I thought I was just hungover. I became so unwell I eventually had to go to hospital to be put on a drip so that I could take in some fluids. By the time I went, I had been alone for over a week, unable to keep anything in my body. I'd begun to show signs of confusion as the result of dehydration, and I'd barely slept because I was vomiting constantly. My mum, without my asking her to, travelled 300 miles and slept on my sofa for a week to look after me as I recovered. Just knowing she was in the next room was like a cool flannel on my forehead. She felt it was her duty to be there, I was her daughter after all. I felt so grateful that she did this for me, but I would never have admitted that I needed her. I would never have asked.

More recently, I had a sudden and inexplicable injury that prevented me from being able to bend my left knee. I was in acute pain, the worst physical pain of my life. After seeing an out-of-hours GP, I ended up in the emergency department at a hospital where I had a long wait ahead of me. My friend Jane texted me, offering to come and join me. I did not let her. I didn't want to be alone, so what use was this martyrdom? I was tired, worried, upset, needed to eat too. She could have brought me some food. She could have just sat with me a while and broken the anxious spell I was in.

I spoke to a therapist about this afterwards, telling them I'd been afraid of putting Jane out, of forcing her to experience something unpleasant: 'No one wants to sit in a hospital,' I said. The therapist told me that by saying no to Jane, I'd denied her the pleasure of helping me. She asked me, 'Would you have wanted to sit with a friend in pain?' I told her I would. Why was it OK for me to help others, but not for them to help me? I had to ask myself about this, about how I nursed my resentment at having 'no one' for whom I considered it to be their official role to support me, at the same time positioning myself as someone who would always consider it my role to help a friend and likely force them to accept it. I realised I was indulging a sense of my own exceptionalism, creating a sharp boundary around what I would allow others to do for me, even if I told myself I could and should cross that boundary in the other direction where needed. If it was OK to ask a friend to be a 'plus-one' at a formal event where everyone else would be partnered, then it had to be OK to ask a friend to attend a less celebratory or even unpleasant occasion with me.

When I returned to the hospital to see a consultant about my injury, Bryony joined me, and when I cried out in pain as the consultant tried to force my knee to bend, she spoke on my behalf. Though I felt a residual shame that I either could not face that appointment alone or that I didn't have a partner who saw themselves as the natural player of that role, I was glad, and grateful, to have her there. And she had the pleasure of being able to help, of feeling needed and useful and kind. I had let Bryony see me in a moment of private vulnerability. Not the kind that can regularly happen between close friends, those moments brought on by rejection, frustration, a missed opportunity, a broken heart. This was intimately domestic. One where my vulnerability could not be concealed. Like clearing up someone's vomit. Remaking their bed when ill.

I still find it easier to withstand another's distress, to be cried on rather than allow myself to cry on someone else. But I am prepared to admit that as I've got older and the distance between my last heartbreak and the present day has grown to a distance that feels unwalkable, there have been times I've lost patience and where empathy had previously flourished, I've found bitterness. My unwillingness to bring my own pain out into the open, to be vulnerable outside of a crisis, meant my pain – contained and pressurised – formed hard edges, and I could no longer think of myself as wholly kind.

When a friend's partner left her, suddenly, cruelly, I found I was repulsed by her grief. Full of dread for bearing witness to her pain, I went to see her. She wailed, 'Is this all I get? Is this all I get? Is this all I get?' I felt aware of a rebuke rising from the mean pit of me – *at least you got this, I've had nothing*. Instead, I held her, saying 'I know, I know, I know.' I did not understand it then, but I had become exhausted by and bored of other people's heartbreaks, how the heartbreak they experienced would cancel out every other thing I saw they had that I did not have. I heard my own internal whine, which had two main grievances: when do I get to be nursed through my own heartbreak, what about me? And then, why are you telling me about this? How would I know what to do? I felt I'd lost my qualification to relate to and talk about love.

I am ashamed of the feelings that my friend's grief for her relationship brought up in me. Not least because all the years I've been single, I've felt my ability to be a 'good' friend has been core to my identity. It has placed me as the person my friends think to call first, the person with the kindest, wisest, most dependable ear. My undealt-with heartache for romantic love had begun to make me bitter and started to impact on my platonic relationships. This has only become clear to me now. At the time I found ways to blame my friends for my emotional responses to their distress, giving myself a pass for feeling overwhelmed. I told myself my unmet desire for romance, and the grief of that, could not hold its own against the brutal grief of my friends' romances gone wrong. I felt so full up of others' pain that there wasn't enough room for my own, as though I had to contain these competing pains in some sort of vessel with a capacity that was fixed. This allowed resentment to grow. Because my ego created a self-image that I was somehow the perfect recipient of others' pain, the platonic ideal of the confidante, I didn't interrogate my behaviour or feelings honestly. And I also refused to let go of romantic love as the one true intimacy, the goal of life. I created much of this pain response myself.

I can see now that I made assumptions about what my friends would take seriously as a source of suffering. I projected my frustration onto them and their relationships, judged them unfairly in terms of their competence – whether they could talk to me about it in a way that would feel 'right' (right being allowed just to have the pain and speak of it, without resolution; right being not confronted with their dissatisfaction with their own romantic relationships, as though the problem was the same). Even today, I've barely spoken of my pain at all, unless ruined by wine, and when that happens, I mainly weep and refuse to divert from any of my rigidly held beliefs that romantic love will always evade me, that I am somehow different in a profound and immutable way. I can so easily conjure the faces of my friends the times I've been in this state, not knowing how to calm me.

There is something behind that belief, the belief I wasn't the same as everyone else. I felt it *underneath the skin*. When I was a child, a man from the church we went to sexually abused me. This isn't something I talk of often, except for when my grief about being on my own spills over, when I'm drunk, or in the company of a woman to whom this happened too. It is frightening how many women this has happened to, and how instinctively we come to know each other. I've had periods of acute emotional distress – a powerful urge to disclose what happened to me – which have brought about searing connections with these women, a sense of psychological intimacy. When someone has been *there for me* or I for them in this regard, my love and respect for them deepens. But these connections don't always last. Sometimes they can feel too powerful, too demanding of a truthfulness that borders on destructive. Every interaction you have goes back to the source of emotional distress, and together you churn it, releasing into your emotional atmosphere feelings you had safely contained. It has sometimes made me feel like intimacy was too risky for me and was one of the difficulties I found with the #MeToo movement. Disclosing traumatic experiences without adequate support can be incredibly dangerous for the still-traumatised person, like living with a pinless grenade.

The experience of abuse harmed me – continues to harm. Part of that harm is the legacy of being asked not to tell. Of feeling my family must have known but didn't talk about it so it must have been OK. But the damage took a long time to show up as something I was able and willing to recognise in my behaviour. When it did, and I broke down in my early thirties, post-traumatic stress defeating me, I got a year's worth of psychotherapy on the NHS. The therapeutic experience was not a good one, but it interested me that in therapy it wasn't the abuse I was moved to talk about. It was my parents' relationship, my own relationship with them, impulsive spending, infatuations with unavailable men, fear of conflict, fear of asking for what I want, my inability to know what I want. I know inevitably these issues connect to unprocessed childhood trauma, create neural maps of cause and effect; even so, it surprised me how little I needed to talk of the trauma. While I thought of the therapy as something I was doing *because* I'd been abused, I powerfully resisted raising the possibility that my terrible childhood experience was the root of my struggle to find romantic love and the sometimes emotionally risky situations I got into with sexual partners. The harm of having involvements where I was not acknowledged or recognised with any status – particularly an affair with a married 'ex' – stripped me of the agency to talk about what was happening in my life, to me, about me. It was a familiar grubbiness, dissociating. I did not want to be defined by what had happened to me, for it to colour my ability to recognise real love, to give and receive it. But of course, it is imprinted on me like Joni's song is for her lover Blue, 'ink on a pin, underneath the skin'.

When I think about romantic love, I can feel stormed by failures. That it is weak to want it. That I've succumbed to lazy, heteronormative ideals of how life should be lived and what relationships and experiences are to be most valued. Misplaced romantic love at life's centre. That it is parochial of me not to valorise the platonic and familial loves I do have and should be more grateful for. Ashamed of how hollow the affirmations of gratitude can sometimes feel to me. I tell myself my aloneness is the result of a lack of imagination and intellect, or that it's pure greed that I'm unable to sustain myself on all the love I do have. I tell myself I am deeply flawed, else it would come to me as easily as I perceive it comes to others. I know that last one at least, that last one is the inseverable tether to my child self. Trust was stolen from me as a child. Some of my earliest experiences confused my sense of love and affection. To a certain extent the abuse I suffered reprogrammed my nervous system so that I was unable to spot a threat, would cooperate with an intent to harm me and read these things as attention, care, love even.

When the abuse had stopped, I remember sitting on my grandad's knee, telling him, 'you can do whatever you want.' He did not do anything; I think he encouraged me to go out and play in the garden. At the time it confused me – I imagine I believed that old men did particular things with young girls, I possibly even felt rejected – but I'm so grateful I was safe with him. I then tried to feel loved in other ways. I remember being seven or eight and volunteering to clean my school classroom's sink during lunch break. It was covered in dried paint and PVA glue. I climbed on a stool and patiently peeled off and then scrubbed the surfaces with Vim. I devoted myself to it because I thought it might make me special to the teacher. Since my childhood, I have had to redefine what intimate spaces look and feel like.

While I have found trusting friendships as an adult, romantically I've almost always felt estranged from trust. It feels like another facet of life that the absence of romantic love withholds from me – a connection with another person so strong you can bear each other's weight intellectually, spiritually, emotionally, physically. The opportunity to do this outside of romantic relationships feels remote, but it feels wrong that that is the case. In a small way, the sea plays this role for me, in its necessary hold on my body, its loosening of what I have kept tight. Because if I have struggled to find someone who I trust to bear the weight of me, someone who wants to bear the weight of me, I can always count on the sea. If I am moving towards a healing in the sense of being more comfortable with my embodiment, more able to integrate my traumatic experiences into my life, it is the sea that I credit.

It cannot be a coincidence that my default anxiety dream is always set at a coastline, an unmapped one; it is never a place I have been or that I know to exist. In these dreams I try to outrun giant, destructive waves. A great fear is the solace of the sea abandoning me.

*

After my thirty-ninth birthday I told myself I would swim in every body of water I encountered before turning forty. I thought it would help with the emotional disquiet of ageing and that 'turning forty' needed that. To be forty years old, without any of the markers of adult life – a partner, a home of my own, a child – made me feel self-conscious in my life, as though I'd not grown into it properly. I wanted, I needed, to grow into my life as it truly was, not as I had expected it to be.

Mostly I kept to my promise. I swam in a tiny hotel basement pool in Cork, in the cave-cold lake Ullswater, a dark plunge pool behind a borrowed house in France where I didn't take my eyes off a river snake on the rocks, various beaches and lidos, and the brisk sea at Ramsgate on the last day of my thirties. The only place I didn't manage was South Shields at Christmas, where I stood alone on the shore, my coat hood pulled up, having left my family to bicker indoors. This practice of being in water – its strange containment – gave me many chances to confront the fears I have about romantic relationships and limerent attachments and how much I mistrust myself. To acknowledge that I enter intimate situations when they're unsafe for me. That I've adopted a position: even if I had a relationship, it would be wrong, with the wrong person, with someone suffocating and fawning, or jealous or cold, or with a person who inspired those behaviours in me. That I've developed fixations with certain men, wanting their approval, their desire, without even being able to say what I admire in them. That I've rebuffed men who have approached me with sweetness.

All around me I look for evidence that helps me feel relieved not to be in a relationship. I went to a poetry reading once, one of those events in crammed bookshops with very few seats. During the poetry reading I had to contain a feeling of disgust and fear brought on by observing a man holding his girlfriend's hand. He rubbed obsessively the skin between her thumb and finger and though she looked ahead to the reader, giving the poet who was reading her attention, the man looked only at her. I wanted to disrupt the reading, *we must stop, there is something terrible going on here*. I wanted to check with the woman: do you consent to this hand? Do you consent to his gaze? I felt sick with it. I felt sick with the idea of *I love to watch you sleep*. I couldn't relax. At one point the woman laughed at a joke the poet made and I felt relief: perhaps this was all OK for her. Perhaps she felt comfort and love, but I imagined the spot on her hand that her boyfriend rubbed becoming inflamed and sore. The skin on her hand giving way. That was not a love for me, I thought. But what would a love for me look like?

Last summer I took Becky on a weekend trip to Norfolk, booking a small beach house just behind the dunes. It had been almost a year since either of us had been in the sea. We got up early to catch high tide and even though it was windy and not yet warm, we walked slowly into the water. It was flecked with a bloom of algae, had a body to it like miso soup that's just been stirred. We sank into the sea, slowly acclimatising to it so it came to feel bathlike. 'I hope we're still doing this when we're old,' Becky said, 'just you and me finding some water and waddling into it.' I felt certain that we would.

I had that private feeling of peace and freedom the sea always offers me, a plunge into my own body. But there was something else, a mutuality. I knew that while Becky and I would swim at our own pace, to our own depths – we trusted each other to know our own boundaries – we would also be watching the other with gentle eyes, one ear held to the shell of the other's voice, so that we'd know when it felt time for us to leave the water together. I realised I knew how it felt to be loved, and that we were sharing an intimacy beyond physical closeness, held together by the sea of course, but also by a kind of faith in our connectedness.

I still wonder, should someone love me romantically, could my psyche take the strain of that, would it let love in? Would I be able to spot the difference between a good and bad love – use the model of intimate friendships to determine what's right? When there has been such a long absence of romantic love, of sex, desire – do I even have a sexual preference for romance to take shape in? Even though I want it all – desire, sex, romantic love – there's a laser trap of questions I put between me and those things.

But there is something in that trap. Travelling up California's coastline I finally acknowledged that these questions exist. That makes me hopeful, not because I need to answer the questions to move through my life, but because the questions I have keep me alert to life as I experience it. I also know that the sea is there to help me neutralise the questions. It's not that they disappear; instead it is akin to noticing another lone bather has entered the water. I meet the other swimmer's eyes, acknowledge them with a subtle tilt of my head. Then I let them drift from my field of vision; I return to my interaction with the sea.

STRANGERS

will you take me as I am?

At the start of my three-week trip to California, deranged with jet lag, I found a cutting of a review of *Blue* on eBay, from a 1971 issue of *Melody Maker*. I hoped I would find some magic bit of Joni memorabilia that would inspire me to write. It only cost a few pounds so I bought it, and it was waiting for me when I arrived home. The review argued that *Blue*'s songs were 'hard to relate to', the 'problem' of the record 'one of empathy'. The experiences cited were 'the sweet dilemma of being stuck in Paris when she wants to be in California' – her ability to fly on a whim to Amsterdam and Rome were 'divorced from our field of experience'. It felt bewilderingly off for me, ridiculous that *Blue*'s lyrics could be considered unrelatable, when I relate to it so powerfully and came to feel that way before I'd even fallen in love; and many years before I had travelled outside of England for the first time. I thought Joni wasn't singing about travel as much as she was singing about finding a way to be herself, to belong within a place wherever it was.

*

In my youth I believed that to go on holiday abroad was to acquire glamour. All it would take was one week in a sunny European resort, an immersion in strangers, and I would be granted access to it. Become liberated from my homeliness, small-town experiences, from the daily sense of making do with hand-me-downs, bland food, the thudding boredom of schooling. I perceived glamour as terrific ease in the world, erudition and imagination, with no labour or artifice to my conversation, mannerisms and style. A polishing of what was latent within. In this way, travelling abroad seemed to parallel the idea I had of romantic love, that it was my destiny, and with it I would step into a truer self. I wanted to be like one of the kids at school, who after a break would walk back into classes with streaks in their hair from the sun, skin pale around their eyes from wearing sunglasses, with the swagger of chaste holiday romances. A temporary celebrity in the playground. My own family holidays were infrequent, domestic and unphotogenic.

I was about to turn twenty-one the first time I left the country. I used some of my student loan to pay for it, my debt already feeling elephantine and pointless to resist. The people I met at university had taken gap years, gone all over the world, had the type of resort holidays I'd idealised as a kid. I didn't always envy their trips – backpacking sounded heinous to me, all the scrimping and discomfort and trust fund babies – but I did envy the broadened palette of experience they had to draw from. They had more colours than I did, and I saw glamour as a richness of expression. I wanted to be perceived as someone who had travelled. I thought that would make me more desirable in the same way I wanted to be thin or have a beautiful singing voice. I thought it might make me more successful at enjoying life. I was convinced it would make me more successful at love. And unlike getting thin, or suddenly having a beautiful singing voice, it seemed a realistic expectation to have. Only money would get in the way of travelling, of the chance to experience different qualities of light, language, cultural norms. I had the same aspiration as my great-great-aunt Mabel – to get beyond the streets of South Shields, where I'd put tremendous effort into changing my accent so I would be accepted.

My friend Anwen and I went to Barcelona by train, and it took over a day to get there. We stayed in a hostel just off Las Ramblas. I had wanted us to get spontaneously caught up in something – a propulsion of alcohol and strangers. But Anwen, less hedonistic, planned for us trips to see the Sagrada Família, Parc Güell, and the Mies van der Rohe pavilion. There she took a photo of me sat on one of his famous white leather Barcelona chairs, a wide expanse of caramel-coloured marble behind me. In the photo I am wearing a white jacket, long wheat-coloured skirt and black shoes. My feet disappear into the black flooring. My body, in its pale clothing and on the white leather chair, glows within the centre of the image, the flash creating a soft halo around my head. Judging by my expression, I imagine my intent was to look serious and dignified. But there is a smile creeping through, the *please like me* instinct too powerful. I had wanted the photo to capture something of me that proved my hypothesis: I was in a sophisticated place, I was a sophisticated person, ready for adult relationships. I'd betrayed myself.

In my twenties, air travel became illogically affordable. It was easy to buy return flights to Spain or Poland or Italy for the cost of a new pair of jeans. I took one or two trips a year – short holidays in European cities like Turin, Bratislava and Paris with friends. But the glamour I thought would break out of me, like a fascinating fossil concealed within a drab stone, didn't seem to arrive. I still felt timid in the places I was in. Insecure and unsophisticated. I'd always be travelling on the cheap, eating emphatically beige meals in my hostel bedroom, drinking so much I'd come home feeling poisoned. I did get things from these experiences though – I became enamoured with the details of places. A spectacularly huge light fitting in the foyer of a run-down communist-era hotel in Bratislava, which looked like a retro schooling aid that would be used to illustrate atomic particles. A meal in Turin, at the point where hunger turns to derangement, of mashed potato and a slice of margarita pizza. The only things my friend and I could decipher on the menu. But I itched for the kind of travel I thought went hand in hand with romantic love. I wanted the staged photos at sunset, every cliché – hot tubs, candle-lit dinners, a personal infinity pool, to suddenly look chic in a wide-brimmed straw hat. I thought this type of holiday was my natural next step. I thought that sort of romance was my natural next step. A progression beyond one-night stands, beyond the constraints of my earliest relationship, where I at first lived at home, then later had a student's budget where even a romantic meal out was unlikely. I ached for the status of relationship that a luxurious holiday would make obvious. In my imaginings I was going to have epic day sex in a white-washed hotel room with the breeze billowing the curtains, sleep with a book over my face next to a pool, carefully adjust the straps of my swimwear to even out a tan. A man who loved me close by with sunscreen or a fresh cocktail. In these holidays, worries, self-consciousness, would fly away, easy as shaking a tablecloth free of crumbs. But this has never happened; in fact, the entirety of my sexual encounters have been in England, something that feels humiliating, as though my sex life has been hopelessly provincial.

It hits now how small and received my ideas of holidaying were. I must have culled them from a magazine or the TV, accepted at face value the flash-shrill photos friends had in frames in their homes. As customary as my notion of which love counts most. Romantic love is the pinnacle of love. Brochure-perfect holidays were what a holiday should look like. I built it up into something it could never match up to. Travelling alone as an adult rather than as a student never occurred to me. I wonder now if it's because that category of holiday was sold to people who'd found themselves alone later in life, after divorce or the death of a spouse. They were sold holidays that would give them a new lease of life after their big romantic love had been lost; were promised new friends, potentially new partners. To be a working-age adult without romantic love at all, rather than one who had love cruelly withdrawn from them, wasn't how I saw myself ending up. Surely only a very unloveable person would have to go on holiday alone.

*

In my thirties I noticed my friends were less eager to holiday with me. They needed to save their holiday time and money to go away with their partners, or with their families so that childcare would be on hand, and I found myself returning to holidaying with my own family. Some of these holidays were difficult – a bad soup of collective mental health problems feeding the family dynamic. Others were placid and sweet. Though I enjoyed being with them, away from shared flats, these trips did not correspond with my idea of what a holiday should be. I'd find myself cooking and cleaning a lot, sleep disturbed by babies and children, slipping into the role of carer – after all, I did want to give the tired parents a break and feel useful and capable. I drew something from my reluctant benevolence.

I had a hunch that it wasn't just gender that created these labour conditions, it was my singleness, my childlessness. In group settings there can be an expectation that the female childless person should give the parenting persons 'a break' from chores for the duration so they can rest. I would find myself aggrieved because, as I lived alone, I did all my own chores every day with the same drudgery as everyone else. I wanted my own break – the opportunity to slip from the dailiness of my life, from always having to share space and be placatory to the needs of the wider group – my flatmates, my family. To take a holiday from what I felt others were looking for from me, and my image of myself within those structures. I didn't want to feel as though I was existing within a hierarchy of who deserved a rest and escapism the most.

There was also the assumption that as a person sleeping alone, I would be happy in a small bed, small room or even to sleep in a makeshift space. I complained about it to my sister once on a family holiday where I had a mattress on a mezzanine level, and people would be walking past my bed as I slept. She snapped at me, 'We have our own room because couples have sex.' In her position I probably would have said the same, but I resented this reinforcement of my lack of status, and the expectation that privacy was not as important to me as it was for people in romantic relationships. *What if I want to fuck myself?* I thought.

At the same time as adopting the mode of carer, I also seemed to regress to that of child, ashamed to have come full circle, back to the family unit. Bratty and sulking at all the compromise of plans, the curtailment of my fun, which would have involved lots of meals out, getting day drunk and lazing on the beach – the sense of glamour I attributed to a good holiday. If my friends couldn't travel with me, and my family holidays were too weighed down by the practicalities of small children and older relatives, I had a choice to make. I didn't especially want to holiday alone, I felt afraid of it. I had the idea I wasn't the kind of person who could holiday alone. Though who that kind of person was I didn't interrogate. But I had no models for it. No one I knew was going away alone without purpose, pleasure being not purpose enough. I also resented the circumstances that made a solo holiday present itself. But I knew I needed to try it to break the resentment I was nurturing, remove the manufactured obstacles from my path. Why did I think only certain types of travel were reserved for romantic love? What hokey reasoning was I basing this on? I knew that someone might think, like that review of *Blue* in *Melody Maker*, I was making a tear-jerker of a 'sweet dilemma'. If a person can afford to take a holiday, why was she so miserable about it? Inventing reasons for why it can't be for her? Making problems out of privilege, like people who turn the good fortune of their wedding arrangements and expensive house renovations into soap-opera-sized vendettas against them. I found my reason one of pride. But this wasn't who I wanted to be.

When I've googled 'solo holidays' I've never seen myself in what is offered. Solo is interpreted as a category defined by singleness, by the absence of romance. The holiday's job seems to be to fix it by introducing you to other 'singles' or sending you on a packed itinerary to distract you from your abject aloneness. Other than that, it's all wellness retreats where it feels like the objective is to come back thinner. I didn't like seeing myself, solo woman traveller, defined as a marketable category, and to find that definition so wrong. All I wanted was the convention of a couple's holiday, quiet, intimate, decadent, but that isn't something they think you might want. I felt I had to build up to my own idea of a solo holiday. At first, I went on a group holiday but stayed in a house on my own, spending the days with the others and then retreating into my own space at night. This felt like a perfect balance, the option to be together or apart. Then I stayed on alone for a few days after they'd left, acclimatising. After that I booked a week's holiday and invited two friends to join me for a couple of days. These were the holiday equivalent of riding a bike with stabilisers on, helping build my confidence for taking off on my own. I found it was easy to be on my own, especially if I was in a self-catering place, somewhere there wasn't much exposure, where no one could identify me as a person alone. I didn't need to work at any kind of self-acceptance because I was removed from being perceived, and that enabled me to stop perceiving myself too. I imagined that as a woman alone in public everyone's eyes would be on me. Or potentially even more of a drag on my ego, that I was melting into the invisibility of non-youth, no longer worth looking at. Something I've had to learn, keep learning, is that no one is looking at me the way I can look at myself, eyes trained on every weak spot to confirm they're still there. These aren't things that occur to me when me and my friends are among strangers. Then I can feel emboldened to be as wretched and loud and silly as I want, because togetherness creates a bubble around our social group that causes everyone else to fall away, to make us believe we're charming.

But I wanted more than the secluded safety of a holiday in a private home, I wanted to go on a *holiday* holiday. The kind that seemed to be preserved for private romantic relationships. I tried to censor this desire, as though it was an admission that I believed in the pretty lies of romantic love – roses and kisses and pretty men. I also felt perhaps I wasn't entitled to it, without a romantic partner, that it would make me more noticeable, more obviously alone.

It was around this time the civil service was planning a major restructure and voluntary redundancy became an option. I felt it could answer my debt catastrophe – my redundancy would likely be a significant sum. If I was able to quickly get another job, I could use it to pay off all my debt and have a couple of thousand pounds left over. That would mean I'd have savings. I'd never had savings. It felt like a miracle. So in January 2017 I left my civil service job, and a month later, started a new one in an adjacent sector. I wanted to mark this freedom, I wanted extravagance. I booked what I thought of as a honeymoon-esque trip, the type I'd seen friends take with their partners, all bikinis, dressing for dinner, daytime cocktails. I wanted to be able to trade in the currency of romantic love and I would purposely insert myself into coupledom's enclaves. I decided to go to Sri Lanka for a week and booked a package deal. Finding a package deal for one is fraught in itself – all the prices are on the basis of two people sharing, and adjusting the toggle on the website to '1 adult' and seeing the price stay the same was a source of grievance. It feels shameful to confess that, given how privileged it is to travel at all – to have the documentation and freedom to travel, not to mention the money, the time. It was a sweet dilemma that I'd allowed – through my self-pity – to triumph over what should have been gratitude.

To go on that trip, to create the momentum I felt was necessary to enter the holiday in the right spirit, I adopted a persona: self-possessed solo traveller woman. A prototype of the glamorous adult I had expected to become. For the first time, I bought myself an airplane outfit – loose-fitting, comfy layers, something that could be slept in. At the airport, I bought a pair of Prada sunglasses, drank a single glass of champagne before heading to the boarding gate. I'd prepared a pouch for my carry-on bag, with an eye mask, ear plugs, noise-cancelling headphones, a lightweight blanket, cooling face spray. The idea is that this preparation helps to deliver you into the holiday as a refreshed, dewy, composed person. This has not been my experience. No matter what provision I make, I feel I enter holidays in a state of derangement. Spillage on my loungewear, my complexion uneven like the skin on the top of a rice pudding, dehydrated from accepting every free wine, a drained phone from too much agitated playing of Candy Crush. My airplane novel unread. But I am undeterred. Each solo trip provides another chance to play the part right, to crack the glamour out of me.

The hotel I chose to stay at was designed by the architect Geoffrey Bawa in the late 70s. It was old enough to have a louche coolness but new enough to offer modernity and comfort without being intimidating. You walked across the threshold of the hotel onto the highly polished floor of the lobby, which in turn leads to a series of interconnected pools pulling your gaze out onto the beach and ocean. It was a beautiful trick of not knowing where the inside ended and the outside began. The horizon effortlessly maintained, and the sky and trees reflected from all surfaces, had the effect of almost disappearing all the material boundaries of the space.

Each night the hotel staff would set up a table for two, with a small beach fire and hanging lanterns, at the apex of this view I first had. They advertised this as the 'where the waves break' table. I both wanted to eat at this table and knew I could not subject myself to the scrutiny of it. Is she a divorcée? Was she jilted? Why is she here alone? These questions were not simply the paranoid thoughts of someone holidaying solo, they were the questions in the minds of the couples holidaying there, who probed me – the *why?* pressing behind the actual questions they asked, the slightly pitiful way they invited me to join them for a drink or an excursion. I did not take them up on it. It can seem an affront that someone would prefer, would find it more enjoyable, to be alone. When I'm sat at a table alone, I wonder how I can indicate to others that I am not waiting to be joined by someone, I don't desire that to happen. I am alone without regret. But it would be better to reach a point where I'm free of thoughts of how others perceive me.

The holiday wasn't perfect. I felt hassled by a man on the beach who wouldn't accept that I did not want to join the excursions he was organising, so I spent a couple of days trying to evade him. Another time, I visited a spice and herb garden. It was full of beautiful, interesting plants – the kind of place I love to spend time in – except the man who showed me around kept referring to my body, telling me about how various herbs would help to prevent the fat in my body from crushing my internal organs. I told him to stop talking about my body, that he was upsetting me and ruining my experience of the garden. It took some hours that day to get over the feelings of self-hatred he had brought on in me. I suspected he would not have said those things if I had been with someone else – it felt personal, intrusive. But I was proud of myself for speaking up, for telling him I was not comfortable, for staying calm. I have so rarely done that, and knowing that I could helped me move on from it. It didn't infect all the days that followed in the way it might have done before. Perhaps travel was less about glamour and more about developing the confidence to know I could look after myself in new, unpredictable environments. I hadn't realised glamour meant the ability to adapt to changes, to find ways to communicate in difficulty, to make myself heard when there's noise I cannot control. It turned out glamour was an action, not an aesthetic. It was glamorous to make my own arrangements, to pay my own bills, to decide when to stay and when to leave. To create my own rules for pleasure. Perhaps I was more glamorous than I thought.

After spending all my days in swimwear switching from pool to sea to sun lounge, most nights I would dress for dinner, and then eat in the hotel's à la carte restaurant. I would order a set menu of mutton curry with various vegetable dishes that changed each time – beetroot, potato, cucumber, spring onion, green bean, paneer – and deep-fried bread that puffed up like an enormous dried seed head, all delivered on a trolley and transferred to crowd my table. I liked this restaurant because it was usually empty, the larger one on-site offering an international buffet that was part of an all-inclusive package. I had a feeling that to eat at a buffet alone looked more tragic than eating at a restaurant alone. The stigma of eating alone in public and my visibility as a fat woman amplified by the abundance of a buffet, its invitation to censor my appetite. Even though I had the props of the solo diner – a novel and my phone – I would usually just look out across the pools of water as I ate, softly pushing my thoughts into the horizon like they were paper boats launched onto the sea. Without a dining companion there is an imperative to appear occupied, kept company by something other than the reliable companion of hunger. But unless your meal is one that can be eaten with a spoon, or with one hand, it is hard – practically speaking – to read and eat at the same time. When I attempt it, I barely get through a sentence without having to set my book down so that I can pick up a knife. As I sat there, the only person alone, I noticed the couples seated at other tables, barely talking, phones in hand. They relied on props too. I began to think about how a holiday needed to involve a tapering off of the grasping part of myself, scanning the environment, the moment, for distraction – a person, a paragraph, a push notification. Letting myself go to the point where I could be content just to sit, to enjoy my meal, notice the effect of different tastes on my senses.

It felt to me I'd experienced this holiday as an actual holiday, rather than going through the motions of a holiday in the hope I could trick myself into experiencing one. I took myself as I was – that meant following my instinct for rest over adventure and accepting that, rather than seeing it as a failure that I wasn't exploring this new country. I just wanted to sit with my little drink, reading my little book, swimming then drying off, then swimming again. It was only towards the very end of that holiday that I sent a message to Becky to say I was beginning to feel a little lonely.

*

Because Sri Lanka had gone so well, because I felt I'd accepted myself there, identified what I needed from that holiday – not a lot other than to sleep, swim and eat nice food – a couple of years later, I splurged again. This time I paid for the trip on a credit card, retreating into the familiar dependency of debt. I told myself this was my reward for reaching forty, for passing the threshold of middle age. I went to Phú Quốc, staying at a small resort in a beachfront room so that I could be in the water in moments. I would swim in the sea after breakfast each day, then in the afternoon swim in the hotel's pool in between reading and drinking cocktails. Then I'd have another sea swim, shower, dress for dinner. After I'd eaten, I'd read in bed before going to sleep early. I didn't need to do anything else, I only sought the recalibrating effect of being in and close to water, for the slowing down and contraction of my days to a small number of activities, and in that slowdown, a quiet would settle within me.

For the last few days of my trip, I booked into a fancy hotel at the other end of the island. I saw this as a big finale, a fortieth birthday treat that would ensure I left the holiday feeling relaxed, worthy of luxury, rich. I've rarely stayed in hotels, and when I have it's usually been for a brief work trip in a neat, functional room. But this hotel was opulent beyond anything I've experienced. I didn't know how to play it cool, to act as though I was at home with the customs of a luxury lifestyle. Without practice, I wondered, would I be able to recognise and perform the coded behaviours of romance? Neither the trappings of luxury travel nor romantic love feel instinctive to me. Coming to the hotel, leaving behind the small resort and its me-sized status, felt like a serious error, as though there were conventions of status and class I'd not been let in on. When did you tip, and how much? What would be given freely and what should be paid for? What failures of etiquette might give me away? I felt anxious I was going to be caught out as an interloper.

In my suite there was a marble bathroom looking out onto a small courtyard garden. I videoed the deep bath running, water pouring from a marble plinth that hovered over it, and sent it to Becky who responded with excitement. I took a bath, drinking Riesling as I lay in it reading my book, and then I took a shower so that I could wash my hair, sitting on the marble seat built into the wall. And I swam. The hotel had numerous pools and I tried them all. One was shaped like a shell with a mosaic of mermaidy blue-and-green tiles. It felt designed for couples, intimate, with romance implicit in the duos of sun loungers placed discreetly away from other pairs. I swam to the underwater ledge at the scalloped edge of the pool and curled myself up there as though against someone else's body. I wanted to cry. I tried to cry. I knew if it came it would be a kind of climax, my body would lurch in ways I was not in control of. I did not cry. The pool was empty, and cloud had temporarily concealed the sun. In that sudden, temporary dark, I had one of those moments of bold thought that you feel might change you forever: I would never be loved in the body I am in by someone I could trust with it. I had never felt loved in the body I am in. How could I enjoy a shell-shaped pool when I didn't know if I would ever feel loved? I was desiccating from the lack of it.

For the rest of that day, I lay on a sofa under an awning, out of public view, a fever coming. I felt that all the riches of this holiday had no value if I had no one to share them with. Did I want a witness to confirm how unsuited I was to a five-star life? Or did I feel a five-star life was reserved for people who have the momentum of romantic love behind them, someone with whom you could laugh at it with, jump up and down on the bed with and conspire with to acquire more than your fair share of complimentary toiletries? At the end of this trip, I posted a photo from my hotel room to Instagram. The photo is of my laptop screen, a carton of chips and a dish with little plastic pots of ketchup and mayonnaise on it. In the caption I wrote 'I have had enough of being a person alone in public'.

It reminded me a bit of my mum's story about her honeymoon. My parents had gone to the New Forest for a few days to stay in a hotel. It was the first hotel my parents had ever stayed in. On their wedding night my mum ordered lobster – another first. But worn out with the stress and commotion of the day, she developed a migraine and could not enjoy any of it. It's a story I've heard many times over the years, a parable about what can happen when you get something you think you want. I still feel as though my mum thinks she doesn't deserve nice things, that even if she gets them something will go wrong.

There was one time I was away, and everything felt just right. But I let myself give in to a sense of being perceived. I was staying in a small seaside town and had been eating in a harbour taverna each day and cooking for myself in the evenings. I'd heard there was a posh restaurant a street away from my B&B. I asked myself if I'd been lazy, just doing the same thing each day, and in that asking booked myself a table for dinner. The restaurant was long and narrow, and I was seated right at the back on a table that was positioned at the head of the room, as though all the other tables were guests of my own table. I began by ordering a sparkling wine, followed by a bottle of orange wine – paying no mind to how these might complement the food. I've looked back at the photos of the food ordered and I'm unsure what I ate. There was something deep fried – arancini possibly – an elaborate assortment of breads, a ceviche and a trio of deserts. I remember feeling disappointed by the food, preferring what I'd eaten most days at the more simple restaurants.

Just after my first course arrived a young woman was seated at a table alone and we nodded at each other from across the room. Before my dessert came, she began speaking to me, asking me if I was on holiday there, where I came from, etc. Since the tables were slightly too far away from each other for us to have a conversation discreetly, I said, 'shall I join you?' and she beckoned me over. The waiter moved my bottle of orange wine to her table. It had seemed a tremendously romantic, exciting thing to suggest. To see a stranger across a room and make the impulsive decision to spend time with them. I rapidly developed a cinematic narrative for the role this meal might play in my life – across the table from one another we might discover something of ourselves.

It did not take long to realise it had been a mistake to join her and to leave the safe and somehow more elegant territory of my own table. We chatted awkwardly. Still, I felt I'd thrown so much money and ambition at the situation I stayed until she finished her own meal, and I ordered a dessert wine, keen to go through the motions of lingering even if we would both have preferred to be alone. We wished each other a good holiday and I took the remains of my orange wine back to my bed and breakfast, where I drank it and sat with a debate in my mind about whether it was good to have tried to make a connection even if the risk did not pay off. I had a feeling that in joining her table I'd given up my hard-won poise of a woman content to be alone in public, betrayed an eagerness to give it all up the moment the chance came. I wanted to feel what it was like to eat in a fancy place as a pair, to see what felt different about it.

Some of this comes from how it can feel to attempt decadence alone. On my trip to LA, just before I came home, I found a last-minute table at a place I'd seen recommended. It was an early sitting, but that suited me. I could go and enjoy myself and then get an early night. When I arrived I was greeted warmly and with enthusiasm and I felt good, as though I embodied a joyful and confident aloneness. I ordered scallops followed by steak and chips. I wanted pure decadent 'date night' food. I was fussed over by the waiting staff. But as the meal wore on and the restaurant filled up with couples and groups, I began to feel invisible and couldn't catch the attention of any staff to order a dessert, to top up my water, to bring back the wine menu. Sometimes in this situation you can see staff are harassed and other diners are struggling in the same way you are. But this wasn't the case. I saw I was less valuable as a table for one. The bill would be smaller, the tip too. The noise I could make less aggressive. I felt myself retreat and my pleasure slow from its earlier gallop. There's a reason people dining alone sit at the bar, it's easier to catch attention there. But I don't want to sit at the bar, on an uncomfortable high stool, my legs swinging. I want the generous *take your time* intimacy of the booth.

Public space is not designed for a person on their own. Private romance and the family are the units by which leisure is parcelled out. I want for myself and for others bars with generously sized individual booths, a little locker to stash your valuables while you use the bathroom, a light you can switch on and off to read. Beautiful spaces that liberate you from the tyranny of togetherness. I want to eat in restaurants with the same abandon I would were I dining with another, or with a group. To be able to order a generous meal for one when the dishes are served 'family style', so that you too can be excitedly greedy without being wasteful. A large range of wines in half-bottles. An assigned person to keep safe your lounger while you go for a swim. A discreet 'I'll take your photo' service so you get to remember how you look when relaxed, happy, taking pleasure. Sunscreen you can magically apply to your entire body without assistance. For me at least, holidaying alone often means getting burned.

Sadness comes out differently when you're on holiday. There you are, in a lovely setting, freshness in all you encounter.

But then the things you're sad about intrude. You meet yourself in a place you hoped might displace your sadness. But you were wrong, and now you're angry too. Sometimes when I'm away it's like I have a devil on my shoulder determined to make me have a bad time, who gets irritated at being made to wait, wounded by poor weather, furious when lost, whiney about choosing somewhere to eat. I have to outwit this devil. Jolt myself out of it. There's a scene in the film *Shirley Valentine*, where Shirley asks a taverna owner to make her 'soft little dream' come true – to move a table and chair to the edge so she can sit by the sea and drink her wine. The sun is going down. The holidays I've taken always include a version of this, the sea being integral to my definition of them. Shirley speaks to camera and talks of the many times she'd pictured herself sitting there, drinking her wine by the sea, but in the end, she doesn't feel at all 'lovely and serene'. Instead, she feels 'pretty daft' and 'awfully, awfully old'. That's how I felt in the ludicrous hotel in Phú Quốc, as though my performance at splendour was seen through by everyone I encountered and especially myself. Splendour had the effect of intensifying my loneliness. The pretty scenes of holidays have to be paralleled by an emotional state that can enjoy them. Getting the timing right is part of it. Setting realistic expectations is another. At first, Shirley desires to be another woman and hopes the holiday will enable that transformation to take place. You can't take leave from yourself. Being away from home alone is a daily exercise in self-acceptance, in taking yourself as you are. Clarifying what truly feels pleasurable and desirable, rather than what you think you ought to seek pleasure in. By the end of the holiday, she's abandoned her normative life, not for love, but for herself. She swaps out her purple housecoat for a silk dressing gown, begins her day opening large windows with the sun shining in. When her husband travels to persuade her to come home, you can read her lips telling him 'I'm not coming home' as the end credits begin to play.

It strikes me that Shirley learns to take herself as she is, to identify her wants, her worth, and she puts it into practice. Maybe that's what Joni is really singing about. When she asks, 'will you take me as I am?' perhaps it's not the place she's asking but herself. I realised in Phú Quốc I'd second-guessed what I needed from a holiday. I didn't need luxury. I didn't need the choice of five pools to swim in. I needed sunshine, yes. But other than that, what I most enjoyed was somewhere comfortable to rest, some water to swim in, and delicious, unfamiliar food to eat that was prepared and delivered and cleared away by someone else. In that environment, I let go, my shoulders drop. Place things about my room as though I own it. Forego underwear and make-up. Sleep as much as I want rather than feel I've failed at being on holiday, at 'making the most of it'. I had to let go of a fantasy I'd created, one that was about having the appearance of someone with romantic love – their confidence, security and glamour – because I thought that was how I would look and feel if I were in love. As though I'd be a completely different person. The ridiculousness of that idea, that fantasy, only visible in the moments I try to express and embody it.

*

I've noticed that since living alone, solo holidays don't have the same appeal they once did. They don't involve a liberation from a shared home environment, where I would rarely have the place to myself, and they have lost some of the revelatory power that comes with the sharp contrast of being around strangers rather than familiar people. I want to find a way of recreating that feeling, but I'm not sure how to do it. Last year, on a solo week in Somerset, I felt miserable and alienated, as though I was hiding out somewhere to escape the consequences of a shameful act. I kept mainly to my rented one-bedroom cottage, watching TV on my laptop sitting in the single love seat, and eating my meals in private gloom, no seasoning able to lift what I cooked. On a dark, clear night I wondered what the stars were like, even though I felt stupid for wanting this soft little thing, so I stepped outside, and into a large puddle, getting my slippers wet, not realising it had rained. A floodlight came on automatically, ruining the effect further. When I got away for another week at the beginning of autumn, I booked somewhere in Essex large enough for a couple of friends to stay so that I wouldn't be alone for all my time there, and then when they'd left, rather than the calmness that sometimes follows being alone after togetherness, I felt restless and afraid. I came home early. Who was I trying to please by staying on longer than I wanted?

When I'm away, no matter how enamoured I am with the place I'm visiting, I am reminded of all I value in my home. I become meek with gratitude for what I have. My ordinary life's rhythms, the shrubs and perennials growing in my garden, how they age with me. The intimacy of living with my cats, their desire for touch and my comfort in touching them. My enjoyment in their goofiness and quirks. When I am travelling back, and reach the final leg, a bus or taxi from the station to my flat, I sing the chorus of 'California' to myself, substituting the word 'folks' for 'cats'. I know I am lucky for the ease with which I can leave and I'm lucky I am always happy to come home.

When Joni repeats 'will you take me as I am?' with evolving emphasis and ascending pitch at the end of 'California' – each pushing at a different vulnerability–I wonder which of the variants is most persuasive. Which variant of me will succeed in taking pleasure from travelling alone – there's 'still a lot of lands to see'. I've attended many occasions alone. Weddings, big birthdays, funerals, dinner parties. When these have been in England, I've often felt anxious, embarrassed even, to be there on my own, drunk too much to displace my awkward feeling. I've found that on holiday alone it is possible for me to slip from a self-mandated veil of shame, one that berates me for failing at being partnered. Sometimes beneath it, I've found confidence, entitlement to a world designed for pairs. The persona I create for the journey receding because it is no longer a mask I'm wearing. I've become.

If I'm no longer escaping to take time for myself, I need to centre my travelling around all the other pleasures that are there to be taken, all the things that reliably 'give me back my smile': my skin turning brown, stopping to notice how pretty the tiles are on an old building, European supermarkets with fruit and vegetables stacked beneath misting apparatus, fancy Californian supermarkets selling fiddlehead ferns and seven types of lemon, meals of vivid coral-pink sea urchin spaghetti, deep-fried baby squid, wilted mountain greens, crisp golden triangles of panelle, pistachio cream doughnuts, the free shot of something sweet and strong when my bill arrives, my body after I've showered off the sea, adopting the same seat each time I return to a bar that becomes 'my bar' for the duration of a holiday, the pride I have that I can holiday alone. If you want to take pleasure in a holiday alone, you need to speak up very directly, identify and pursue your desires, protect your boundaries in ways you might not have to in company, because no one else will advocate for you and there is no other flow to go with. The cost of not doing this is discomfort, displeasure and a feeling of wastefulness. This can mean striding into a restaurant and asking to sit at the table with a good view, having won over an impulse to be subservient to a couple who might see me 'taking up' a table intended for two. I've found myself feeling guilty for not being active on holiday, not going to see great landmarks or on excursions when I'd rather rest. Finding the sweet spot between gently pushing yourself to do things that could be wonderful and allowing yourself to do absolutely nothing takes work and practice. A holiday should include a break from self-punishment, as well as a break from work and the expectations of others.

I've just returned from a week in Tenerife, my first out-of-the-country trip since LA. It made me smile when one of the waitstaff at the hotel said to me, 'hey I love your style – eating alone, with your bottle of wine and your book and your nice blue shoes.' I had ordered a bottle of wine from her to eat with my meal, asking to take it back to my room afterwards. I'd wanted to get into my pyjamas, have a glass of wine and watch TV in bed. I'd taken my habits with me. I inch towards my holiday persona, who doesn't have movie star glamour, who isn't concerned with artifice, but is in communion with her own wants, needs and pleasures. Even if I know a timidity might set in, as though all my powers of aloneness have been spent by the heroic act of arriving elsewhere, on every trip I relearn how to be alone. I'm still travelling, travelling, travelling.

CRAZY

can't numb you out of my mind

In 'This Flight Tonight' Joni is flying away from her lover, full of agitation at leaving him behind. She jumps from thought to thought – worrying about whether his car got fixed, plunging into the 'blackness, blackness' of despair, recalling sex 'down south between the trailers', love gentle and sweet, thinking of his 'look so critical', fretting if he is warm enough. She wants to drink, numb, drum him out of her mind, but she can't. She's a hot/cold discord of love, lust and longing, the melody hopping up and down in register, mimicking the feeling.

When I think of my romantic life, it's this kind of panicked, anxious desire I think of, a near crazy feeling. But while you're allowed to be crazy for someone, your romantic craziness – the texts, body language, the expectations, dates and declarations – must be requited. If it's not, you are quickly relegated to your object's league of lovers or exes who were crazy, forever ridiculed and caricatured to friends and future partners. In my experience my endurance in the crazy stage has often outlived that of my object of attraction. They've withdrawn reciprocation without warning and left me reeling, my behaviour towards them suddenly gaudy and misplaced. I try to summon the qualities that had appealed to the love object in the first place – a pert intelligence, a spooky alignment in tastes and interests, a hair style they'd admired – and go to desperate lengths to make sure they notice. But I've been left waving at someone who pretends not to see me, as though they've begun a game and forgotten to tell me the rules. Then I wind up feeling *crazy* crazy.

*

An unavailable man I slept with over several years once said to me, 'You're not going to do anything stupid like fall in love with me, are you?' We were sitting in a beer garden, an hour outside of London. I'd taken the afternoon off work to meet him where his barge was moored. He'd kept me waiting for him at the train station where he was due to pick me up. He'd texted me while I was on the train to ask me to take off my underwear. I'd been so compliant. His question-warning made me protest: how audacious to think I might love him! But it was no use, he'd already seen me. Seen how my eyes were moonstruck for him. I had no idea how to guard my ardency, to keep him alert to the possibility he could fall in love with me and lose me. But the way he'd said it told me it had never occurred to him. Now I cannot locate a scrap of what I admired in him; I can no longer be certain which ancient romantic injury I am still needling, and what losses have made me so scared to feel.

When I first met him, I was twenty-four. It was as though someone had restored the power to a whole fairground, and as the bright lights blinked into life, the throb of electricity set off an alarm of desire. To borrow Joni's words, he lit up 'this poor heart of mine'. I'd never had my chemicals respond so powerfully to another person, a person who, had someone shown me a photograph of them, I would have felt no impulse of attraction for. I thought this was *it*, the wild pulse of living through romantic love I had prepared myself for. I knew instantly I would have sex with this man. I didn't know how it was going to happen, but I had no doubt that it would. When a week later we had sex at his house, I told him of my premonition, and he found my presumption very funny. Some years later, when we talked about that first time, he admitted to me he'd had the same feeling. We both just knew. Just knowing was something people in love seemed to sense. When both our bodies felt the same, how was it that I thought it was love and he knew it wasn't? The contrast of our emotional responses can still baffle me.

This relationship internalised the idea that romantic love had to involve a dramatic sexual attraction. From then on I paid no attention to weaker attractions – I would not allow and was not interested in the possibility that feeling might grow. Romance had to be intolerable and addictive, it had to have the magnificence of a falling star burning up the sky, to hold within it the precarity of passion's end. If I couldn't sleep, couldn't eat, that was *the* real thing. Near constant agitation for someone's attention, someone's sexual interest, that was *it*. The seemingly involuntary action of another body in response to my body was how romantic love came to be defined for me, in part because I'd not experienced since my late teens the other ways romantic love (its shared fandoms, mutual fascination, love notes under pillows, its hand-holding, its shared plan-making) might be expressed. It feels like we readily accept that there can be sex without love, but we're less open about romantic love without sex, or romantic relationships where sex isn't prioritised. Coupled people joke about how their partner only 'gets lucky' on their birthday or Christmas, affairs happen because sex has absented a relationship and someone's hormones are activated by a new attraction. It can't help anyone that romantic love is so idealised.

I couldn't believe it was better to be alone than to be, as I described it at the time in relation to the unavailable man, 'half alone'. In a no-man's land of status. My diary from that time is full of lists – self-improvement, bills and debts, aggressively melancholic playlists, imploring commands to stop contacting him and 'see what happens'. I find it painful to read what I chose to record of me and him, beyond my desperate need for more. I didn't write about us fucking in the woods in late summer, or how powerful I felt in my stockings as he walked up the stairs behind me while pulling down the long, cold zip of my dress, in a way I had designed, or of how potent his desire was for me – but how I warmed my cold feet on the soft hair of his belly. What I wanted to record were the scraps of tenderness in the larger fabric of our sexual relationship, and through that, magic them into something larger, more significant: signs of love. Surely, I thought, these are signs of love; I can take cuttings and make them grow.

That's the trickery of bad, unequal relationships. You can believe you've given so much to someone, you can't afford for it not to work. All my life I've spent time in seaside arcades, drawn to the penny falls games, where you put in pounds and pounds' worth of pennies and tuppences for the exhilarating cascade of the coins to tip over the edge and into the tray below. The tipping point of believing I would get a return on the investment of love I'd made, and the giddy pleasure of receiving anything, masking how poorly I'd invested. I wasn't prepared to accept that I was fuckable but not loveable.

At the time I thought our sexual compatibility was incredible, perhaps in part due to our hunger for it. One time after having sex he played me a song called 'She Loves My Cock', about a woman who would 'walk through the flames of hell to get to my cock'. I laughed and said 'well, maybe up Highgate Hill'. I remember being on a bus once, on the way to Finsbury Park station, and a man and a woman got on. They were incredibly high. The woman shouted repeatedly to the man, *I wanna fuck, I wanna fuck*, grabbing at her crotch with a frantic appeal to her partner, desperate for relief. I was disturbed by how inhibition had abandoned her. I also understood. I thought about sex constantly.

But I am nagged by a reality. Because of my inability to sense and speak of what I most desired, even after many hours of sex, even though I was turned on, I often left his bed unsatisfied. I would ask him 'do you like me?' and he'd say 'evidently,' gesturing to his cock, but what I meant was, do you *like me* like me. I wasn't honest with him about the potential scope of my feelings, about my desire to be fixed in place by him; instead, I felt like a spinning top, propelled into action through him. This saw me not sleeping in case I missed a message from him asking me to come over, ditching my friends to take long, expensive taxi journeys to his flat, falling from the back of an old London bus while it was in motion because he'd texted '?' to me and I had to change direction to reach him. And when his interest failed, which it frequently did, my behaviour became a stumbling waltz of humiliation as I tried to regain his attention. The spinning top faltering.

Our initial involvement lasted eighteen months or so. We barely ever spent time in public together, until he disappeared on me, having met someone he married and had a child with shortly after. Someone whom he had in fact met the day we last saw each other, his likely attraction for her temporarily displaced onto my willing body. I'd felt his excitement that night, him pulling me onto his lap in the kitchen so I would abandon the meal I was preparing. All his talk of the conditions not being right for him and I to have a relationship evaporating like the illusory mist it was. The last text he sent me, the day after he finally picked up the phone and explained that he'd met someone else, that he was in love, said 'Sorry for being a cunt.' I waited until I was alone in the work toilets and then sobbed. I couldn't call him a cunt even after he called himself one, so powerful was my self-deception that I didn't love him, that I had no right to be angry. After I composed myself, I replied, 'I wish you well.' I didn't know what gaslighting was, I had no language for it. I felt furious with myself that I could fathom a relationship out of thin air and find myself heartbroken when it was taken away. For me it was all I could think of. For him it was nothing.

A couple of years later, when that relationship faltered, he texted. I was in a different job, a different office, and seeing his number on my phone, one that I had memorised, made me throw up. I agreed to meet him. After a couple of hours in the pub listening to him list all the problems in his marriage, and his regret at how he had treated me, we walked back to my front door. He followed me in and up to my bedroom. As soon as the door was closed our hands and lips were on each other. He begged me for more, and I felt powerless to it, my desire as strong as ever. Some small part of me believed that going through the pain and humiliation of an affair with him was a necessary evil to finally secure his love and commitment. That this is what it had meant to be 'prepared to bleed' for love.

Now I read the wild pulse I felt when I first met him as terror. My absolute giving over to desire and submerging the sense of self I'd so tenderly created, and my shock at just how tentative my identity was, how subject to the forces of another – it could collapse like a soufflé. I could only contain the sense of my want, its effects on my physicality, rather than the substance of it, the ability to name what it was I wanted. My dad had a long-term affair while married to my mum, and to have an affair felt abhorrent to me, not necessarily because I moralised about affairs but because I did not want to be like him. But when the time came, it was disturbingly easy.

Overnight I reprised my role as object. Because our relationship was wholly sexual, I sometimes felt abstracted into parts. Breasts, ass, lips, cunt. It felt hot that elements of my body could inspire in him a kind of delirious worship. But also alienating. More than that, this time I wanted tenderness and care. He was not interested in giving it.

Because we saw each other so irregularly, I'd spend hours some nights taking nudes, sending them to him and waiting for his nudes in reply, staying awake half the night. This was before smartphones, so the ability to capture a good image took a lot of patience. If he wanted one when I was out, I'd think nothing of leaving my friends waiting for half an hour while I'd go into a pub toilet cubicle to take photos of my breasts and wait for his reaction, his request for more. I preferred my friends to think I was taking a particularly terrible shit than to admit why I'd been gone so long. I'd pull out of plans at short notice because the opportunity came up to see him. The promise of his attention toppled anything and anyone. I kept this up for almost two years.

Things ended when he told me he and his wife were having another child. The fantasy of what the affair meant, and how he'd positioned his relationship with his wife (inert, over), was detonated by this news; where once there was a towering feeling of magnificent romantic difficulty, now there was only aftermath. His wife, who I'd never met or even seen a photograph of, became a real person in my mind. I told him to stop contacting me, cutting myself loose from the leash of an arrangement that did not serve me.

He didn't stop contacting me, but I stopped responding. The sudden exit of my desire was surprising. It was as if a medication had been switched and my symptoms had disappeared. I didn't think too deeply about why, I just felt relieved that I'd found my boundary at last.

This particular man is probably the most central of my romantic relationships, simply because he is who I had sex with over the longest time frame, but he is also emblematic of many more. Of how many times I attempted to stretch my sexual partners to fit a template of romantic life that I desperately wanted. At a house party I once took someone I'd just met to bed and after we'd had sex and fallen asleep, I dreamed he told me he loved me, and I woke crying realising this hadn't happened and wouldn't happen with him. Another time, taking home the guitarist from the band who played my work Christmas party, I again ended up in tears when he revealed he had a girlfriend straight after I'd made him cum. I'm unsure whether it was because I'd pinned a dream onto him specifically, or if it was how quickly the possibility of something beyond sex was nixed. It was always the same story – I was hotly desired, but not for long. Elsewhere, a more refined, less eager woman waited. I waited too, my need humming like a fridge at night, for someone to touch me and quiet my wanting.

When I was younger, my paternal grandma, Eva, would often ask me if I was 'courting'. I almost always said no.

Though we had a warm relationship, she could turn on people very quickly, and I wasn't an exception. One time, when she was at our family home for a get-together, she asked the question again. Again I said no. A whisky-spite in her voice, she said 'you drop your knickers too soon.' I spat back at her 'how would you know?' and left the room. Her words hurt me. I'd already internalised that I was only good for sex, that sex was how men would show they liked me, but it would also disqualify me from being loved. Most of the time I took what I could get rather than wait for what I might eventually get. I took issue with the idea that a boy wouldn't take me 'seriously' if I slept with them straight away. It was misogynist. So even though I experienced that behaviour – being sorted into a category of *only for sex* from men I hoped for more from – I rejected it as a reality. But on an emotional level – in the realm of my magical thinking – it also didn't make sense to me. I felt confused that someone could want to sleep with me and leave, that someone with my strength of romantic feeling, what I even perhaps considered a kind of panache for it, should not have love. But still I carried on having sex and making myself available to have sex with people who *did* have romantic feeling for others, as though the outcome might end up being different. It is still a source of genuine bewilderment to me that for the majority of my sexual partners I have been a kind of fun, erotic diversion prior to their commitment to another woman who more adequately met their brief for partnership. I also felt angry at myself that I couldn't simply enjoy sex for sex's sake.

In the house we lived in when I was a teenager, I would sit on the toilet, the only room in the house with a lock, staring at the wooden door, and each time I'd notice in the grain of the wood the eyes of a creature I might find in the wild – a fox, a rabbit. Every time I noticed it, I would remember all the times I'd seen it before, but I did not enter the toilet thinking *I'll say hello to the eyes in the wood again*, I seemingly discovered them anew, felt beguiled by them each time. It has been the same with men. My habit has been to notice each time I gave more than I received, but this self-knowledge did not help me anticipate it, to translate the knowledge into different decisions, different actions. What was, what is, wrong with me?

I sometimes, in an absence of composure, asked men I knew. Often their answers were banal – my expectations were too high, I was intimidating, or if I would just 'stop looking' love would come along, as though love needs the element of surprise to make its entrance. Once, high, I asked a man I barely knew, and though I can't remember the exact words he used, he told me that this pleading search for love was visible to men, and that threw me – what could they see and why was it so off-putting? Surely, I did not want love in ways that were so peculiar, so repellent that I should be denied? It suggested a memory from my childhood where my father flared up with rage because he was unhappy with the way I held my fork. He was disgusted with me, and it was unacceptable: I must change. It confused me – it was only a fork, but clearly it symbolised so much more for him. A lack of grace perhaps, a slovenliness that did not fit with his idea of femininity. Sometimes I still grab a fork or a pen in the same manner – all fist – and in my mind I'm weaponising it.

*

In my early thirties an acquaintance I knew through mutual friends began to give me a lot of attention, sending me sweet and funny messages, creating in-jokes that suggested a deep, shared personal history. I'd known him for a few years but didn't have any strong feelings about him, any particular attraction, in fact I'm pretty sure I'd noted his presence before and thought he seemed young and a bit of a prick. But within a couple of weeks of his attentive and, as I read it, flirtatious communication with me, I was deep into an infatuation I felt no ability or desire to climb out of. He was with someone in those early weeks, at the tail end of a long relationship, and I mistakenly believed he wanted to be with me when it fell apart. He bought me a present from a trip he'd taken with his girlfriend, an antique hip flask, secretly handing it to me under a pub table; chatted to me late into the night online; made plan after plan to be in the same place. I read all this as romantic intent. I had butterflies for the first time in years, couldn't eat, or sleep. I thought it was love growing in me; it was hungry and wild and insatiable, like my stomach had teeth and was gnashing them constantly because I refused to feed it. When he and his girlfriend broke up, I said he could stay at mine. I wanted him to. I wanted to be around him all the time.

My head and heart felt full of something reactive. Sometimes the sensation was pleasant like sherbet, thrillingly fizzy and sweet/sour, my mouth suddenly filled up with it. Sometimes it was frightening – as though my vital organs were responding to a poison, causing my breath, pulse and brain to become choked up and fail.

Rosemary Tonks is one of the first poets I loved. At the time I came to know her she'd been out of print for decades. I was sent a PDF of her poems that had been typed up from original copies of her books and had been circulating by email for years. What struck me about her poems was how repulsed she was by her own romantic desires. To Tonks, love was a calamity to be survived. A 'half-erotic' opportunity for loathing. She has a poem called 'Badly Chosen Lover'. She addresses said lover: 'My spirit broke her fast on you.' The words seemed to go through me, left me awed as though I'd got too close to a ferocious waterfall. I'd waited so long to be loved I had to eat. Our way of being with each other seemed to have the marvellous rapidity of mutual obsession. That giddy version of achieving emotional closeness which in adult life happens most often in love. I felt I was going to get my person. One night on the bus home a girl overheard our sparky back and forth and said, 'you two are so cute,' as she got off the bus. We had quickly established a common language – pet names, shorthands, silly voices. I loved feeling in it: a private, secret, covetable world. I stood in the full beam of his attention, and it was glorious. I felt beautiful, interesting, hilarious, cute, clever, a good cook, a good fuck. I felt briefly invincible – all my nerve endings were shrieking with life. I knew that love could do that. I'd seen it happen.

I wanted love so badly I persuaded myself things were present in our relationship that were not. Every word of rejection, denial and disinterest was reshaped by me into something more ambiguous, more promising. I told myself that the fact we were having sex, that he was staying with me, made what he said about his feelings towards me unreliable. He was kidding himself, not me.

This delusion was so powerful, it utterly disarmed me of any defence I should have been able to marshal. I felt like I was at the arcade again, dropping silver coin after silver coin into the machine, waiting patiently for my rewards to come. I worried about what he was eating, preparing meals and boxing him up leftovers to take to work. I imagined myself as a wife, coy and quiet. I took to drinking the same drinks as him, wearing vintage clothes I knew he liked. I cut my fringe back in. I tried to become smaller. I was contorting to try to meet an image I could never replicate. As quickly as I felt the full power of his gaze on me, he turned it off again, moved on to multiple other subjects. I lagged, still stupid with love, a soft old dog trailing behind the new puppy. I hadn't even noticed how nasty he was, his cruelties operating in stealth. Most of the women he courted he did privately, a couple he did right in front of me, getting furious at me for being upset about it. It was just how he'd designed it. My reality was a collapsible, frail thing. One evening I joined him at some birthday drinks for a mutual friend. Someone I'd known for a while, but was not close to, leant over to me and said, 'Amy, why are you here when these people are not your friends?' I looked at her idiotically. What was she talking about? It seemed like a mean thing for her to say. But I wish I'd taken it as a warning. In another of Rosemary Tonks's poems, 'Done For!' the speaker urges the reader to beware of what might happen if 'you make love to the wrong person [. . .] / You'll lose your identity, and never get yourself back'.

That's what I felt happened to me in only a few months. I cried so much over this relationship, what it did to my heart and head, I felt the skin on my face might become see-through and fragile, like a wet tissue. So many people saw me cry during that time, garish and scrambling for something that did not exist. I was disintegrating in public, with no idea how to recuperate.

The affair I'd had in my late twenties caused me a lot of pain, but I don't think it fundamentally shook me from my identity in the way this short involvement did. One reason for that is when the affair ended, I'd only just turned thirty.

I still felt an optimism that there was more romance for me, I felt young enough, desirable enough, to grab it. I kept having sex when the opportunity arose, believing someone would stick, someone wouldn't be able to get enough of me, would be the cat who wanted to settle in my lap. As though I might be able to attach to them so lightly, so imperceptibly, like a burr on a jumper after a walk through the woods, that they wouldn't feel moved to shrug me off. I wanted to be invisible to them in some way, something emollient, all the while feeling out of my mind with desire. I think I would have kept doing this had it not been for the disastrous involvement with the badly chosen lover.

In an interview with *Rolling Stone* in 1979, Joni said, 'The *Blue* album, there's hardly a dishonest note in the vocals. At that period in my life, I had no personal defences. I felt like a cellophane wrapper on a pack of cigarettes.' This romantic experience scraped a layer from me. I didn't even have the protection of cellophane. I felt a heartbreak of shocking intensity, grandeur even. I was voluble, uninhibited, laid out my pain across every channel. It wasn't even for him, for how humiliating it was to see him enter a very public relationship with a mutual friend (and consequently realising how hidden he'd kept ours). It was a heartbreak brought on by how lost I felt: I'd not cared for my 'one child'. My 'cherished self'. I thought I'd pushed so hard for his love that love itself skittered away from me with the force of my action. In my situation of putting romantic love at the centre of life, I not only rendered all other loves subordinate but also placed myself as subordinate to other lives.

As I was coming to terms with this loss, I kept up a cordial relationship with the catalyst for this pain. But I wasn't the same person I'd been before. I was brittle, paranoid, leaking emotional content. I had to turn away, protect my nervous system from a love/hate addiction. I deactivated my profiles, withdrew from the places I might encounter him. Before I knew it, I'd cut him off so sharply he may as well have been struck by the blade of a guillotine. The cost of getting it wrong, the cost of this attachment was too great. And because I felt I could not be trusted to differentiate sex from love, I also shut off from its potential pleasures too. Fear drove this, but it was also a different kind of risk I took: if I cut myself right back, like a rose bush, perhaps I would grow back stronger. By Christmas of that year, I felt scooped up enough to throw a party in my tiny basement flat, instating a new personal tradition. It was an act of faith in the future possibility of if not love, then joy.

A few years later, in the surge of #MeToo disclosures, a woman contacted me – on behalf of a group of women – to ask if I had experienced sexual assault, coercion, violence or emotional abuse at his hands. I read the message in a supermarket car park and let out a howl of pain that felt primal, the absolute pitch of horror. I thought I'd been the only one harmed by him, harmed because I was weak, lacked self-esteem, was desperate. Harmed due to my own negligence and tendency to settle. The other women had experienced even worse. My grief for what had happened between him and me was displaced by grief for everyone he'd harmed. I had been so fooled I never spotted how dangerous he was. I thought I might have been able to stop him.

*

I used to identify myself as some kind of patron saint of unrequited love, but there have also been men who felt unrequited love for me. One of those men was Roddy. I don't think I was very kind to them. I'm not innocent, I've been both victim and perpetrator of shitty relationship behaviour. Thinking about the men who wanted to be with me, I slept with their friends, pretended not to understand when they talked to me about their feelings. They were left unheard and invalidated. I did not want to actively cause harm, but I did. I was a coward, unprepared to take responsibility for my feelings and actions, and I was too devoted to the unstable impulses of other desires. I was always terrified these men would make a move on me because I found physical declarations even harder to loosen myself from.

It's strange to think that the boyfriend I had when I got pregnant at nineteen was one of my first boyfriends but also one of the last. The last *official* boyfriend, i.e., the last one who referred to himself as my boyfriend, was the one that came a little while after. That last relationship began its ending on the first day of the new millennium. We were staying at my sister's in Manchester, after an anticlimactic party. I didn't want to have sex with him, my attraction to him having dwindled, and so, quietly, without much of a disagreement, he left and went back to Leeds where we both lived at the time. That same morning, I found a ring he'd given me on the floor in two pieces, the amber stone come loose from its setting. Looking back on my diary from that time was revealing. I wrote often about feeling suffocated by him, being repelled by his declarations of love, loving him but not feeling passionate about him, finding him pathetic. I was shocked by my cruelty. I'd written, 'God, men must have felt this way about me a million times and it's awful.' Suddenly empathising.

Recently I've been thinking of how my own stories – my own sexual history – have achieved a kind of obsolescence, as though they're examples in a textbook that now feel laughably out of date. I remember when I broke up with my first serious boyfriend, after he stole my parents' wedding rings. He was distraught, and I was immediately cold. He begged me to stay with him, wrote me letters, threatened self-harm if I didn't take him back. After a few weeks I had little patience for it. I didn't think he was a bad person for stealing, he had a lot of problems that I likely didn't understand and I just wanted to move on. He was with someone else a month or so later. About ten years ago he sent me a message on Facebook saying, 'Sorry for ruining your life.' I assured him he had not.

Every so often a new yardstick occurs to me. I have more important people in my life named Rebecca than I have had romantic partners. In the time I have been single one of my friends has had three long-term relationships, been married, had a child, got divorced and is now in another serious relationship. I am chastened by these thoughts, as though I've been stuck in time while others have grown up. I resent how culture can conspire to make single women feel as though their lives aren't 'real' enough. For me, there's been no meeting the parents, no mutual *I Love You*s, barely any first dates. No being handed wine in glasses with stems as tall as a pint of beer before cosying up on the sofa to watch the next episode of a favourite show. No conversations about how to spend the summer holidays this year. The man whom I'd had the affair with, when I was sleeping with him before he got married, and who insistently was not my *boyfriend*, once came back with me to my family home at Christmas, but in the dead of night after we'd met friends in the pub. He snuck out without being seen the next day. He would bait me. 'You want me to say I'm your boyfriend or something,' he'd sneer. 'You want it on a certificate or something.' Only once did I have the courage to say, 'yes!'

*

The last date I went on was with a poet in his seventies I had no intention of becoming romantically involved with. He sent me postcards and called me on the telephone. After dinner at a place near to where he lived, he invited me over to his museum-grade house – a time capsule from the 50s – with no central heating, no internet, a fabulously and unintentionally stylish dishevelment. He went on a lot about having no money, but since he lived in a three-storey house in a fancy part of London I didn't pay a lot of attention to that. His *no money* wasn't the same as another person's *no money*. We sat in the basement by the warmth of an ancient portable heater, the kind with bars that glow, drinking cups of peppermint tea. I didn't want to stay too long; I felt a little drunk and had to get up early. When my taxi arrived, he saw me to the door and kissed me on the lips as he said goodbye. I couldn't register what my body thought of it. A few months later, after a lot of free wine at a poetry event, I invited him to come home with me and kissed him in my bed with the lights off. I kissed him absolutely free of desire for him, let him touch my breasts. I realised I should not see him again, in part because I didn't trust myself to rebuff his romantic attention, and that disturbed me. It had happened before.

My romantic and sexual encounters have included moments, days, weeks, occasionally months of joyfulness or, if not joyfulness, memorable experiences. When the pickings are so slim, it can be easy to disregard the nice bits. I remember one boy in my early twenties, an art student from Portugal. I only met him a handful of times. In my memory he looked like one of the Strokes, skinny, dark hair and eyes, unstudied worn-in clothes. I wrote in my diary that he had a 'puffy face'. I thought he was beautiful. We left a party somewhere in south London and were both heading for London Bridge, where we would go our separate ways. But when we got there, we bought some cans of beer and went down to the Thames and sat drinking and talking for hours. At 1 a.m. I asked him to come home with me. He was into Charles Bukowski and after I met him, I bought some of his poetry books. And then I signed up to a poetry class. When that class didn't get enough people signing up, and they closed it down, the teacher suggested I transfer to Roddy Lumsden's workshop. I'd never heard of Roddy but a week later I walked into his classroom. I'd decided that if Bukowski could be a poet I could too. This boy had led me to Roddy, to starting to write.

Before he and I kissed for the first time, the boy said 'you are a very nice girl.' He said it slowly, a talking-in-his-sleep mumble but his eyes in touch with mine. The kissing and sex part of our encounter was clumsy and unremarkable, but the whole evening is drenched in romantic feeling for me. I never saw him again. I want another night like that. That look in a person's eyes just before they kiss you, I want to see that again. A kind of thickening of the atmosphere, as though you've entered personal mutual weather conditions. I remember one time, out with friends in Brighton, a friend of a friend turning slowly on their heel, wondering whether to kiss me. I didn't notice in time. You never imagine you've used up all your life's eyes-before-a-kiss moments. Very occasionally I feel a theatrical stab in my heart, *I don't want to live if they're all gone.*

When I was a young adult, I remember saying to friends, 'I don't need a man to validate my existence,' again and again as though forcing myself to smile because I once read that smiling will actually make you feel happier even if you don't feel like it. Now, as I approach my mid-forties, it seems it's taken all this time for it to become true for me. I don't need someone's romantic love to be validated – if I look at my life as it is, it's a good life. But I also want love. And I don't want to just make do, scrape off the surface of a burned piece of toast.

As I've been writing this book, I've allowed these men to spend time once again in my mind, a temporary unbanishment, and they've bled into my dreaming life too. I've woken to dreams of good sex. Bodies and sensations collapsing in on each other. Tuning out – everything being felt at once. Tuning in – everything distinctive, small, fascinating. Beautiful disorientation. Regret at waking then shame at the feeling I'd regressed into active emotions I'd left behind.

But then I've woken from bad sex. Trying to fuck someone into loving me. Trying to argue someone into loving me. Sex without eroticism. Sex without care. Sex without desire. Sex without consent. Relief at waking then shame. Or there's been no sex. Instead I've woken distraught at an emotional entrapment I thought I was rid of. In the dream, rejected and enticed and manipulated.

I have tried to get through my days with the residue of these Frankensteinian experiences with men I used to know still stuck to me. These have been the cruellest of dreams. My brain's way of saying *ha! You thought you were over this! I'll show you!* My body's way of saying *you'd still want to fuck him, you know. You'd fuck him right now*. 'You'll lose your identity,' says Rosemary. 'Can't drum you out of my mind,' says Joni. I try to shake the dreams from me like I would a spider, screaming.

I thought I had to create a bulletproof mental state before attempting to love romantically again. I couldn't risk the chance I might, in further acts of recklessness, stash my self-esteem within a person who could fundamentally damage it. I couldn't financially, physically or mentally afford to feel crazy again. I didn't absent myself from desire during this time, I think I redirected it – into things (creation of home), into projects (writing, learning to garden, taking up painting). I kept desire channelled into less risky ventures. I thought that if I felt a hellish anguish for a relationship that had no status, that was barely there (thinking about how I could explain 'barely there', a line from one of Roddy's poems occurs to me: 'Think of the palest pale blue – paler / than that'), how could I tolerate losing a good love? One with tangible, material edges and arrangements to connect my life to another? I no longer think that. I can see that romantic love isn't something you can postpone forever; it has no perfect conditions. I will never be invulnerable to love's power to avalanche the self, I just hope I'm better at identifying the risks. But I've not yet been able to connect that knowledge to a positive action.

When I was seeing a therapist a couple of years back, she asked me to write a list of what I would like in a potential partner and to bring it to our next session. I was round my friend Ella's house for dinner, and she offered to help me with it. Even coming up with a list of things that were important for me felt hard. Some of it was the defeated part of me that assumed I would never get what I wanted – being madly desired was something I felt was important, but I also knew it had to be less important than it had been in the past – but some of it was simply not knowing. Ella wrote things down as I thought out loud. I remember saying 'someone who goes outdoors' and 'someone who is enthusiastic about something' – my bar set very low. But a lot of the other things I said were borrowed ideas from positive representations of romance, or just too generic. It made me think of a list Roddy once wrote when I asked him why he liked me and how it didn't have a specificity that made me feel seen, it was all 'blonde, curvy, likes music, Geordie' etc.

It was probably a mistake to try to write my own list at that time. It didn't seem credible to me that I could name my terms. I think part of that is because within my own experience thus far, I don't know if the things I want are the things that would satisfy me; I haven't had a chance to try them out. But I want to be loved. I want the bruised mouth of kissing after breaking the fast of kisses. Tracing my lips with my fingers days after the kissing's end. I want to wake to love notes on my phone on my fridge on my bedside table enacted into eggs and toast and orange juice. I want to feel sheer with desire, all circuitry and membrane. I want to feel out of logic and routine and responsibility. I want to feel a private cosiness next to another body in public. I want to stop someone on the street to ask *can you take our picture?* I want more voltage. I want so much I've never said it.

Instead, I have wanted to be changed. To become or resemble an ideal of someone's romantic partner, always looking within myself to identify what it was that got in the way of love, the tiny adjustments I could make to fulfil another's vision. My eyes were so trained on my own imperfect state that I failed to consider the imperfection of the romantic partners I sought. If I think back to the man I had the affair with, the desire for him to *like me* like me – to see me as valuable to him beyond sexual pleasure – was so strong I didn't even ask myself if I liked him. Once the spell was broken, I realised I didn't. He would text me now and then over the years since we were involved, telling me he missed me, talking like friends. There was no friendship there for me. He was boring, arrogant, talked down to me. And who would blame him when I so clearly placed myself in service to him, failed to stand up for things that I desperately wanted, became oddly characterless in the face of his personality.

I've periodically downloaded Tinder and Hinge. Every time I get a notification from Hinge that tells me a man likes me, I rebut them in my mind with *I don't think they should!* I've thought, half joking, about joining a kink-based app where I could attempt to find someone who considers extreme long-term single people incredibly hot. *WLTM someone un-freaked out by my history of romantic loveless-ness*. I'd like to reduce it to something that feels as acceptable as my other unattractive qualities: not eating fruit before it goes off, cutting corners cleaning the fridge, or hogging the mic at karaoke. Like Joni, 'sometimes I think love is just mythical'. Sex, I miss, but I'm aware some of the things I might want from a romantic partner are infantile. Someone to be able to be a brat to without consequences, someone to baby me with soft words and the tucking in of a blanket when I feel vulnerable and unwilling to be accountable for myself. I wail that if I don't get a romantic partner, I'll never spot that lump that needs to be checked out and then die. Then other things I want are more than equalled by my closest friendships – emotional intimacy, making plans for the weekend, for short trips, for things we want to celebrate, and the foundational support of curiosity, feedback and encouragement that helps the people we love go after things they want.

In my earliest years of writing poetry, a tutor once asked me 'what do you want to be?' He meant, as a poet. I found the question a bit too grand, I didn't feel equal to considering it. After a while, I said 'I want to write great love poems.' But what I meant was, I want to be loved. I still do. I want to feel someone's eyes on me as I sing Joni songs while driving the car, and for them to think to themselves, without saying it, *I love her, I'm going to kiss her*.

LOST

I wish I had a river

The awful heartwork
of it and I'm saying, shamefully, aloud, here on the balcony

that I love you as if still there were a teasing plenty, when, when

teasing plenty is gone and that, *that*, beyond my stash of chance.

Roddy Lumsden, 'The Nevermore'

The first time I met Roddy, in his poetry class, he struck me as one of the most awkward, particular people I'd ever encountered. Someone once described him to me as 'the most himself man' they'd ever met, and that felt startlingly correct. I did not feel relaxed in his company for almost two years. I remember my surprise when he told me he always felt happier if I was in the same room as him, that it comforted him and made him feel at home. It felt like cognitive dissonance, that someone who manifested as so awkward around people, was in fact not feeling awkward.

Roddy's kingdom was the pub. After every poetry class we would go there, and even though he did not lead the conversation, he held court, each student taking turns to buy him a drink. We all wanted to have a moment with him, hear what he thought of our poems, whether we were any good. He had favourite students, and that created its own dramatic tension, but his taste was broad; he was interested in all kinds of poetries and people. He offered all of his students something – the exquisitely formal poet, the blazing spoken-word poet, the absolute beginners and the bored returners, the working-class writer who'd always been left out, the bawdy octogenarian, and my own category of student: the young woman reaching back to rescue the creative impulses of girlhood. Each of us looked to Roddy to help us inch closer towards really being in the world. That was the talent he had. We all drank a lot. We played pool, put songs on the jukebox, ate Scampi Fries, went through phases of smoking and not smoking, asked Roddy to test us with his quiz questions. I felt for the first time since my late teens a release into a community of sorts, a social scene that orbited around him, and slowly we became friends, sharing music with one another, sharing a love of contemporary US women poets, sharing close friends. He was the perfect teacher for me to have found. Not just because of what he introduced me to in poetry and how that fundamentally influenced my intellectual and creative life, but the way in which he took his students out into the world, made them write poems for elaborately conceived events, put people together. At his invitation I wrote so many (bad) poems on unlikely things – one about rugby (he'd assigned poets a topic 'not like them'), another about the 'Greased Lightnin'' dance move, another one about New York when he asked fifty poets to write about one State each. At that stage in my life, twenty-seven, I really needed it. My friends were mainly paired off and into their serious work of mutual future-making. I was trying to figure out what my own future might involve, and Roddy helped situate not just poetry in it but also new friends.

I began to hang out with some students from Roddy's class outside of poetry events, in a small workshop group where

Roddy would come along after we'd all swapped poems, to drink and eat with us. Through this I developed a close friendship with another classmate, Camellia, who had known Roddy for a few years already. At one workshop, she did my make-up, painting a mermaidy blue/green on my eyelids, just before I left to go on what I thought was a date (it was not). At the end of another, we went to a pub in the middle of Bow, a true regulars' pub where we were tolerated rather than welcomed, and we sobbed in silence listening to a mum and daughter sing Elton John's 'Sacrifice' on the karaoke. It was a romantic beginning to our friendship. I loved that Camellia loved Roddy and seeing the playful, sweet interactions Camellia and Roddy had made me fonder of both of them. There is a photo of the three of us from those days, Camellia and I either side of Roddy and him looking delighted by it.

Roddy went on to edit both of our debut pamphlets and poetry collections. We launched the books together at a huge party, an occasion that seemed to celebrate our relationships to each other as well as the books themselves. He gave us both gifts to mark what we'd made together. Mine was a 'Luxe Cat' – a small plastic cat he asked his flatmate to turn into a brooch for me. She had painted it yellow and stuck diamantés on it, like the cover of my book.

In the early years of our friendship Roddy made me mix CDs, which is one of my own favourite strategies for showing someone I care. I still listen to them now. Music was a faithful, expansive channel into which our relationship could flow. Our tastes didn't precisely align, but that was the fun of it. We would listen to some bands in joint rapture – the Field Mice, Heavenly, Lavender Diamond. Other songs, beloved by one of us or the other, we would mercilessly pick apart, as though looking at a poem by someone we did not rate. He once told me he'd listened to sixty-seven versions of Joni Mitchell's 'Both Sides Now' and the Skeeter Davis version was the best. On that we did not agree. He hosted 'records night' where he would invite a handful of friends over to play songs each of us chose aligned to ten different categories. Through this he introduced me to the song 'The Leanover' by Life Without Buildings and when I hear it now, I am back there a decade ago, near vibrating with awe at it. I threw parties at Christmas and on my birthdays for all the poets I knew, and Roddy and I would always decide to *do a number*, making everyone listen to us sing Deacon Blue's 'Loaded', or 'Dignity', him taking the male vocal, me the female. He didn't know this, but they were a band I listened to a lot with my older siblings, and in singing those songs with me he was recreating happy memories from a childhood where there were few.

We kissed a couple of times. The first time was an end-of-night blur, standing in the street after the pub had closed, rounding off a soul-wretched conversation, one where I probably asked him why romance was eluding me. A little after, he was at my flat for an editorial meeting. He asked if he could kiss me and I said no, and he said he had to leave because he was 'heartbroken'. I felt terribly embarrassed that he'd asked me, and also deeply uncomfortable that if he'd just kissed me, I wouldn't have declined – I've always struggled to not respond when a move is made. The second time we kissed, I was aware of taking advantage of his attraction to me. I felt sad and rejected by someone else, and I wanted to see if he could dislodge my bad feeling.

Roddy had successful relationships from his teens up until his early forties. And after those, he was always falling for someone, in thrall to the dramatic potential of a crush: unrequited love a necessary fuel for his creative expression. His books are full of evidence of this. Often, I'd tell him off about mooning over another young woman in his poetry class – he was the type of man who didn't believe he held any power whatsoever, even though he was the 'big poet'. He was always older, in a position of authority, but refused to believe that he had more status than a beautiful younger woman. 'She's the one with the power,' he'd exclaim, with irritation. We often fought about this. When I challenged him about the appropriateness of an infatuation or his interpretation of a younger woman's behaviour towards him, he would accuse me of being jealous, because 'after all', he said, 'we have a history'. I was not jealous, but there was likely something else at play there that I did not convincingly know how to voice. The fact that when Roddy and I met I was twenty-seven and he was about to turn forty, so my desire for him to think more critically about his interactions with younger women was borne of experience, not just of the early quasi-romantic evolution of my relationship with him, but of how I'm always seeing older men, men with status and power, interacting with younger women.

When I had my flat in Peckham, living alone for the first time, I would often invite Roddy over on Saturday nights. The poetry events we pegged our social lives onto were most often during the week, when pubs would offer up their rooms for free. As we were both single, weekends could be lonely, and I'd not yet learned how to enjoy being alone. He'd turn up with booze and snacks, and we'd cook and listen to music, and he'd entertain my cats, whom he adored, and we'd gossip and talk about what was tearing at our hearts. In this way, Roddy and I ended up kind of as friends with benefits, where the benefits were someone to cook with and cook for rather than fuck. We performed domestic intimacy, preparing simple meals for one another, the fanfareless meals I imagine exist in cohabitation – soups, stews, curries. The first time I cooked for him he told me, 'this is the food I like to eat, and it is the food I like to cook,' and I took great pleasure in getting it right, as though I'd picked for him the perfect gift.

Often what was tearing at our hearts was what he described as 'the givers of crumbs', romantic objects that made us feel grateful for the other's scraps of attention. He could stay up talking for hours, and though I loved the stories he'd tell me, quite often I'd end up having to tell him to go home because I was falling asleep. I'd order him a taxi knowing he'd probably stay awake drinking for a good few hours yet, and I might wake to poems he'd sent me, written while I was sleeping.

One Saturday afternoon Roddy called me. He was crying and said he was at a pub nearby and could he come and see me. I said he could. He told me that he had realised he was an alcoholic and that he wanted to stop drinking. Roddy's drinking was something I had noticed but never talked about to him. Most times when we were out, we would stay until last orders and on the way to the tube Roddy would always buy some cans to have when he got home, or if he was around at mine and I called it a night, he would get a cab back to his local, concerned to get there before last orders. He recounted a conversation he'd had with an American poet who'd visited London recently. She had stopped drinking and said to him, 'Roddy, I am happy. I am HAPPY for the first time.' He had a stunned look on his face, he wanted this for himself. He told me the previous weekend he'd tried to stop, supported by his flatmate, but after only one day he'd experienced delirium tremens, including hallucination, and had felt terrified he was going to die. Sobbing, he said, 'Amy, I want to be happy.' I said I would do what I could to help him. I felt proud of him for his courage. It was the only time we spoke of alcohol being something he wanted to be free of. After that, if drinking came up, he might talk about wanting to cut down, or switching to lower-alcohol drinks, but he didn't identify with alcoholism and quickly shut the discussion down.

Two years later I was at the launch of Roddy's latest poetry collection. I noticed Roddy's trousers were soaked through at the ankle, as though he had been walking through tall grass covered in dew. I asked about it and he lifted up his trouser leg, revealing swollen flesh and huge pink sores. He told me that he had unbearably itchy skin; that his vision had gone milky. When he drank his pint, he tipped the glass so the liquid fell straight down his neck at speed. I consulted with my friends outside while they smoked. We decided to try to get him to hospital after the reading. He refused, telling us he would only see a private dermatologist and he was going to ask his rich friend to pay for an appointment.

A few days earlier I'd spent time googling symptoms of liver disease. I'd wanted to be able to spot if his alcoholism had begun to make itself visible in his physical health. Having internalised the list of signs, I felt certain it was not a dermatologist he needed. Camellia called NHS 111 who said we should call 999 for a section if he would not attend hospital; I felt Roddy would never forgive us for doing that. We remonstrated with him outside the pub for over an hour. I eventually persuaded him to come back home with me and Camellia to my flat, thinking that from there we could convince him to go to A&E. He sat on the sofa, telling lewd stories from his teenage years. He kept saying the word 'boobies' in his soft Scottish accent, the conversation became silly, playful. He would not be persuaded; we ran out of steam. I ordered him a taxi to take him home to Blackheath. I was convinced he would develop septicaemia and die alone in the night.

Even though Roddy would not allow us to take him to hospital that night, he had no reservations about letting someone feel the full weight of his needs. That's something I've rarely done – literally, metaphorically, I've never felt comfortable enough to let someone take on my physical and emotional burdens, I've resisted being carried.

Roddy wasn't like this. He didn't seem to worry about asking people to do things for him. That interested me because I found it so hard to ask for help, but it made me angry too. From the time his illness became obvious his life began to rapidly unravel and he wasn't able to take any responsibility for it. He had to move from the room he rented because he had fallen out with his live-in landlord. He couldn't find somewhere else to live and eventually a friend from his local pub agreed he could stay with her temporarily. A few days prior to the move I asked him if he had things sorted, he told me no: he needed a man and van, and he was just going to see if any lads from his local could help move the boxes. It was clear he needed help. I spoke to friends – one booked and paid for a removal man, the rest of us agreed we'd go on the day to load up and unload at Roddy's temporary place.

I arrived first. Roddy had done no packing whatsoever. He was sitting on his sofa, drinking from a bottle of cider. He needed to drink to function at this stage, even though it also caused his dysfunction, and he said it helped his pain. Though I found it hard to watch him drink I knew it was dangerous for him to stop. I'd not seen him for a couple of weeks and his physical state was incredibly upsetting, but the size of the task – we had two hours to pack – meant it was dangerous to pay attention to painful thoughts. As others started to arrive, and I let them in, I would caution as we climbed the stairs into the flat – *I need to let you know this is going to be difficult*. There were nine of us. Roddy seemed to just want us to sit and have a chat, with no sense of how much there was to do. We divided the tasks. Roddy said, 'there's what I call the hard stuff,' gesturing to his books, 'and then there's the detritus' (clothes, papers, etc.) I was responsible for the detritus. I was responsible for his bedroom.

I'd never been into Roddy's bedroom before and what I found there was squalor. I felt my jaw clamp as though to suppress a scream and this scream attempted to surge beyond my throat the whole time I was in the room. There was a narrow gangway around his bed littered with crumbs, packets, scraps, and then the perimeter of the room was piled high with bags, boxes, mouldering food on plates – the detritus Roddy mentioned.

I felt in acute distress that Roddy had been living in this way. These were no conditions in which someone might be able to find resilience, hopefulness, or be able to heal. It was horrendous to encounter this frenzy of material evidence of just how bad things were. I'm reminded now that Roddy once asked for my advice after he'd visited the flat of a friend of his, to feed her cats while she was away. He wrote to me how 'her study is now an absolute no-go zone, with many bin bags of stuff piled high. You can barely enter that room.

The bathroom has a big pile of stuff on the floor (again, empty soft-drink cans and bottles, clothes, shoes, etc.), so much that you can't open the door properly.' It had really upset him to see his friend's living conditions – he told me he'd cried his eyes out at the sight.

As we packed and sorted and cleaned the flat, Roddy sat still. He sometimes seemed like a little prince, issuing commands, and sometimes like a scared little boy, looking to us anxiously to reassure him it would all be OK, frightened of losing track of where his alcohol had been put. He was unable to put on his shoes without help as his feet were very swollen, so my friend Martha did it for him. It was only then I let tears fill my eyes, standing back so he could not see.

I wrote to Camellia later that day to update her on how it had gone. I told her the move had left me so dirty that when I drained the bath I'd taken afterwards, a thick black watermark remained. The experience clung to me like a nauseating scent I'd layered onto my body, one that could not be rinsed off.

Between the time we'd noticed his weeping legs (a symptom of cirrhosis of the liver) and Roddy's eventual long-term admission to hospital, a period of about a year, Roddy lost his footing in all areas of life. He was unable to work, he lost his housing, many of his personal and professional relationships were mired in difficulty. From the outside, it would be easy to blame alcoholism for all these problems, but it is never that simple.

Roddy identified as an autistic person, self-diagnosing 'introspective Asperger's'. He believed his brain was 'wired differently' to a normative person and that made sense to me. It helped me recalibrate what I had perceived as failings in his friendship towards me. He very rarely asked how I *was* – he wouldn't participate in the exchange of 'checking in' and I found that frustrating and at times, hurtful. When I asked him about it, he said it just did not occur to him, but that was not indicative of whether he cared or not. Roddy also had periods of mental illness, including depersonalisation and bipolar disorder. In his youth he'd had electroconvulsive therapy and been prescribed medications he felt had robbed him of his identity. From then on, he was deeply suspicious and fearful of clinical interventions that were not strictly concerned with physical ailments. The extent of the contribution Roddy's neurodivergence and mental ill health made to his alcoholism developing or his ability to overcome alcoholism I will never know for sure, but I am certain the difficulties he experienced were the result of the intimate connection of all three. It did not feel like the meagre help that was available to him through the NHS could contend with the complexity of his needs; the health and care system as he experienced it was fundamentally flawed. He had also become very frail, often ending up in A&E due to falls and blacking out. One of his arms had become withered following a shoulder injury he resisted getting seen to. He couldn't drink in the same way, but he needed to keep drinking. I and many of his friends found we moved back and forth along a spectrum of emotional response: deep compassion and patience, anger, vigorous practicality, irritation, denial, grief, hope. But thinking back to that time, to my own exasperation with what was happening to Roddy, I wish I had realised sooner how unfair it was for me to have expected Roddy to have a handle on his life, to manage all its administrative puzzles and demands, and to conform to an obscure social code of conduct when the world can be so hostile to autistic people, people with mental health conditions or addictions. I should have done better.

I learned a lot about myself through this experience – my capacity for empathy was not as boundless as I'd imagined it to be, my patience was inconsistent, I was quick to blame and I was quick to grieve before it became certain Roddy would die from his illness. I began to grieve as soon as I saw those sores on his leg. I remember attending my friend's mum's funeral and in a speech someone spoke about how, when she was in the hospice, she'd instructed those around her to 'only take away the very dead' flowers. It made such an impression on me, my friend's mum's ability to hang on to and appreciate the ailing flowers in the vase, not letting them go until it really was time for them to go.

Sometimes I was a bad friend. Once someone called me at work to say Roddy had gone missing in Waterloo and had locked himself in a pub toilet somewhere and was threatening to kill himself. Though I rallied friends to go and find him, I found reasons not to go myself. I was gripped by a deep suspicion he was trying to manipulate me, recalling my first boyfriend standing in front of me slashing lightly across his belly with a knife because I had wanted to go home. I am deeply ashamed of not always rising to Roddy's cries for help, the ways in which he was able to express his pain. But in the interminable duration of his illness, I felt it was my own self that I'd have to sacrifice to be what he needed me to be, and though many times I felt I was getting close to a kind of annihilation, to becoming lost to myself, I always pulled back. Pulled back and away from him.

The last place Roddy lived independently was in East Ham; at this point there were no good days. Camellia and I made arrangements to visit him. She'd had to persuade me to go. All contact with him made me feel a sickening anxiety. I found myself only able to be devoted to him or completely absent, and these on/off periods were variably stretched, sometimes minutes or hours, sometimes weeks and months. I knew it hurt him deeply when I was not around, but he really struggled to consider how what he was going through might impact another person, and I found I couldn't talk to him about how I was feeling without one or both of us becoming powerfully emotionally activated and the conversation going awry.

Roddy wanted romantic salvation. More than once he said to me it was only real love that would make him live, and that weighed on me heavily, the thought there was something that might fix things. I think he meant it, but I also doubt it would have worked. I remember him asking a question to a group of poets once, which he himself answered:

> Q: Which one of these three is most conducive to good poetry – grief, intoxication or being in love?
>
> A: Being in love – by quite some distance over intoxication, ditto grief – generalisations of course.

The tragedy and melancholy of romantic love had genuine allure for Roddy, and all his loves generated astonishing poems. His last relationship, with a younger woman called Bella, inspired hundreds of poems, which kept coming long after the relationship ended. His willingness to write people's names into poems was, is, very out of its time. He knew some people found it a bit too ardent, or twee, but he didn't pay much attention to fashions. Of the dozen or so poems he wrote about me, or with me in them, only a couple made it into his books and they're easy to spot as he uses my name. There is one poem, though, that he told me was about me even though I'm not named. He wrote it just after we had kissed for the first time. 'Only / when I used up all my nos did I say yes' the poem ends. Roddy wrote a key into that poem, which could not have been without intended associations. When I showed him a poem I'd written about him, about the heartache of his illness – almost a pre-emptive elegy – in order to seek his permission to publish it, he wept and told me all his pain had been worth it to be written about in that way. I am sure he meant that too, at least when he said the words he did.

On the day Camellia and I visited Roddy we waited on the steps of his flat for forty minutes before he was able to answer the door. When he finally opened it he was bent double and crying out in pain. I saw he had no socks on, no trousers, no pants. Shit smeared around his calves, his hands. His feet and ankles were a swollen unit – red, peeling and weeping sore.

What I felt was a haze of rage landing on my body. A haze that obscured where my horror was. Rather than compassion, I felt fury.

We tried to help him inside, there were a few steps to take. He seemed unable or unwilling to take a step, it was the sort of difficulty that does not appear real to another person.

He fell back and though we caught him, held him steady, he wanted to sit on the floor of the communal hallway in his building. He suggested that we go into the flat and wait for him to move, but that meant standing in his flat, which was hot and sweet with evaporating alcohol.

His duvet lay in the middle of the floor – bloody? piss-stained? I felt appalled at the thought of it.

Even in the moment I was asking myself why I was so angry. Was it because he was not ashamed of his nakedness, his helplessness, his need? Or was I angry because of my own shame, because I wanted to be out of the dire confines of his life as seen in that room, and not laying out newspaper for him to sit on as he'd been unable to clean himself properly.

I wanted to leave. I intuited: this is not a safe place for you. He said 'once I get on the sofa, you'll see another me.' Eventually we were able to help him through the doorway and onto the sofa. He smoked a cigarette as though the cigarette were the medium through which he was able to exist. We sat there in silence. Camellia went to the shop to buy some groceries and cigarettes. Each of us wanted an escape – unable to really allow myself to *see* him, I got up and cleaned the kitchen as best I could and made him up a packet of pasta 'n' sauce. He talked in a gossipy way about poets and poetry – he'd been sent dozens upon dozens of books and manuscripts, he said – and he asked me to put on some music, the Innocence Mission, and for a short while things were as they always were. He'd been right in a way – once on the sofa he was 'another' him. After we left to drive back home, I let the physical relief of leaving his flat sit with me for a long time before I allowed the sadness of the visit in.

I'd spend long periods daydreaming of how I could restore him to health through careful management of his domestic life. I daydreamed this as intensely as a lottery win. As though clean sheets, orderly possessions, regular mealtimes and careful observation would save him; if I couldn't give him *real love*, if *real love* wasn't going to happen for him, this might do the trick. Part of me still believes it would have. Instead, this dire need for order was something I placed on myself, to stop my own well-being careering off the tracks. It interests me that while I lack discipline in some areas of my life – spending in particular – I am incredibly controlled in my environmental conditions. I find myself unable to tolerate any disruptions in my routines, in my domestic environment. This desire for control leaked beyond my home – other people's worries began to feel like an intrusion on me and a grave threat to my ability to keep things together, as though I'd have to absorb them, carry them in addition to the burden of my own.

Shortly after this visit Roddy was admitted to hospital, having fallen on the street. His good friend Anne, a student of his who visited him regularly, got in touch to let me know, and told me I should go to see him as soon as I could. I left home immediately and drove there. He'd been placed under Deprivation of Liberty Safeguards, having been judged unable to make decisions about his own care. I was relieved, as previously he'd often discharged himself from hospital early.

A condition called hepatic encephalopathy can affect people with advanced liver disease. It is caused by a build-up of toxins in the body due to liver damage. These toxins travel through the body and affect brain function. Roddy developed it. It gave him delusions, making conversations with him hard to follow and often very distressing. Because I was so frightened that every time I saw him might be the last, after each visit I would write down everything I could remember him saying, and, in doing that, sift the Roddy I knew from the Roddy carried away by his illness. Often he'd be animated by a fantasy that was gripping him at that moment – that he was married to one of the nurses, or that the man in the neighbouring bed was a murderer, or he himself had murdered someone, or that he'd booked us a table for dinner and could I order a taxi? One day, he was in a quiet mood. I was fussing with his lunch, trying to get him to eat. He looked at me and said, 'Love hasn't happened for you, has it?' I was shocked by the acuity and cold blade of his observation.

I look back at some of the other things he said during that time:

> 'How do you feel about me being gone forever?'
> 'You don't love me, you told me my girlfriend is dead!'
> 'I want to come to live with you, but I am worried you will become attracted to me.'
> 'Why are you laughing?'
> 'How do you feel about me dying? We should talk about that.'
> 'I wanted to marry you but that will never happen.'
> 'Your skin is so soft, I can say things like that now.'
> 'You will die like me, only worse!'
> 'I won't compromise! I will not compromise! You won't change and I won't change!'
> 'Can I come and stay with you?'
> 'Why aren't you crying?'
> 'I am going your way, can I come with you?'
> 'Could you just point me in the right direction?'

He said to me, 'Don't think I will stop loving life just because I've stopped loving you.' I asked, 'You've stopped loving me?' And he said, 'No, the opposite.' 'OK,' I said.

I'd often leave the hospital in floods of tears, on the phone to Camellia to relay what had happened during the visit.

One time, the time he told me that I did not love him, and that I was cruel for keeping him there, a woman patient who was outside having a cigarette put her arms around me as I cried into my phone, holding me until I stopped shaking. One arm tight around my shoulders. One arm held away to keep the cigarette smoke from me.

Roddy's delusions often related to girlfriends, wives, weddings and babies. I found this talk more distressing than his delusions of being a murderer or that he was being held 'as part of an experiment' in South America, because they spoke of his true desire and the hopes he'd had for his life. The intensity of these hopes was so powerful that it gave shape to his confused thinking. I felt so sad for him I even suggested to Camellia that I marry him, so that he could at least have that before he died. I always told him I loved him before I left his bedside; one time he said, 'everyone is being so lovey-dovey it's doing my head in.' I had to laugh.

One of the panics that gripped me and friends while Roddy was in hospital was that we might not know his favourite song, what he might choose to be played at his funeral, even though I was certain we'd talked about it one night, late, drinking and playing songs to each other. None of us were able to answer the question, so we agreed to try to find out in conversation with him. During a moment of lucidity, he mentioned Michael Nyman. But everything I listened to took on a doomnote and I found myself weeping most days. Mary Margaret O'Hara's 'To Cry About' called out to me, 'There will be a timed disaster / there's no you in my hereafter'. It felt like prophecy. 'You give me something to cry about,' she sang.

There were so many times during the period he was in hospital when we thought he might die. Living with that possibility was a daily source of tremors. My internal landscape felt volatile and created a sense of being unsafe in my own body as anxiety had overrun it. On one of these days, my thirty-ninth birthday, I received a call from Camellia just before midnight, as my small party was winding down, to let me know Roddy had been stabbed in the head with a pair of scissors by another patient on the ward. Though he was miraculously OK, I let go of months on months' worth of hysterical feeling, crying and raging until I fell asleep as the sun began to rise.

Due to a new medication that treated the hepatic encephalopathy he was suffering with, Roddy was eventually able to be discharged from hospital and transferred to a nursing home. Officially he was being given palliative care – we were told he would not recover. But his frightening delusions ended. Again, we could talk to each other, his brilliance and mischief was back, and everyone who visited him came away staggered and thrilled by his transformation. But this meant he also now had a real understanding of the graveness of his situation. Hope came with the possibility of a liver transplant and a shortlisting of his final book for the T. S. Eliot Prize for Poetry. He was incredibly proud – Roddy never doubted his own talent and this recognition was taken with real pleasure rather than faux humbleness or disbelief. This self-possession regarding his writing was so pronounced I ended up feeling impressed and occasionally amused. He began to talk of organising readings, perhaps teaching again. He spoke into the future, and it was beautiful to have those conversations. But he did not win the prize and was denied a liver transplant. After that he became smaller and quieter. All the things that made Roddy so alive – music, food, puzzles, crushes, poetry, gossip – lost their animating power. He watched TV in his room, sometimes made it to the garden to smoke a cigarette; the number of regular visitors dwindled.

Once again, I became avoidant, finding my own visits to him excruciating. It was hard to make myself really look at him with eyes free of fear, judgement, anger, grief. He wouldn't let me put the lights on or open the windows – the atmosphere in his room suffocated me. I alleviated my guilt by telling myself he did not enjoy my visits. I kept track of his biting remarks about my poetry, my relationships, mutual friends, the extent to which in his view I'd been good to him or not. I needed reasons beyond my cowardliness. But in truth, I'd lost my courage and wanted only the comfort of leaving and not being left. This failing in myself caused as much distress as the visits did. I wish I'd made a different choice. His brother Eric, his friends Matthew, Anne and Mark, kept up their weekly visits. I am left with regret that I did not bear witness to his final weeks; I did not have the endurance and compassion they had. I did not want to be touched by his humanity because to allow that meant connecting to the brutality of grief. Because of this I slipped from the top of a list of who would be informed when he died.

On New Year's Eve 2019, I was content to be spending the night alone in my new flat. *My flat* gave the aloneness a particular allure. I pulled three tarot cards, the question in my mind, *will I ever have love?* Six of coins for the present, ten of wands for the past, death for the future. That night I went to bed before the clocks struck twelve. I tried to keep my interpretation of the cards open. A profound loss might be coming, I did not assume it was a death. What would I have to give up? What might be taken from me against my will? Ten days later Roddy died.

The night it happened, I was with my friends Amy and Bryony. We were watching videos of Canadian figure skaters

Tessa Virtue and Scott Moir. One in particular, their final (gold-medal-winning) Olympic performance, beguiled us. It led to a conversation – a game almost – about what music we would each skate to for our 'short' and 'long' programmes. My friend Amy knew immediately: she would skate to 'Video Games' by Lana Del Rey for her short programme, and then 'Permafrost' by Magazine for her long programme. We were drinking and got distracted by another line of conversation before Bryony and I could think about our own answers.

When I woke up the next day, I rewatched Virtue and Moir in bed, tears slinking down my face. It came to me that I would skate my long programme to 'River' by Joni – give myself a real river 'to skate away on'. I played the song, visualising a routine. As the song ended, I went onto Facebook to send the ice-skating video to a friend who I thought would love it. It was at that moment I was told of Roddy's death, via a notification in a group I'd helped set up on Facebook to coordinate help for Roddy and share news privately.

I had imagined receiving the news of Roddy's death many times before it happened. When it did, alongside the horror of my grief, which felt like an emotional and bodily landslide, was my panic that because I was alone, I might die of it before Becky, who I had asked to come, had the chance to get to me. I felt like my breath was battling against my grief. It hijacked my lungs, heart, veins, throat and mouth and ears. It seemed impossible any breath could enter or leave. I had always thought I wouldn't know who to call when Roddy died, as though there was no one nearby who could take that immediate weight of witnessing me in my distress, but when it happened, I did not hesitate. Becky arrived, held me as soon as I opened the door. I remember her kissing my head, stroking my hair. I remember how small I felt, ready to be mothered by her. Ready, for the first time, to let the whole weight of my sorrow rest on her.

The fear I would be alone when I found out he'd died was borne out, but it turned out that it barely mattered. Nothing could have made it easier. I am glad no one is left with the memory of the sound I made. I wish I had a river. I loved him.

At Roddy's funeral I struggled to explain the nature of my relationship with him to his family. It troubled me, and Camellia that we had no status as mourners, no official title we could bestow on our relation to Roddy. The best I could come up with was that it was not a romantic relationship, but that it sometimes had a romantic dynamic. I ask myself what that dynamic consisted of – some of it was the *hate you some, hate you some, love you some* feeling that I'd schooled myself to expect in my relationships with men. We really wound each other up; Roddy would often feel rejected by me, and I infuriated by him. But we had something. We shared the same favourite poem called 'Project for a Fainting' by Brenda Shaughnessy. In the poem the speaker says, 'Would I dance with you? / Both forever and rather die.' Now, when I read that line, I tie it to Joni's 'I hate you some, I love you some'. We loved to talk food. We loved to talk music. The first time he signed one of his books for me, he wrote 'no end and no beginning'. I knew it was a reference to me dancing to Madonna's 'Like a Prayer' early on in our friendship. But those words pulled from that song seemed perfect: the sense you've always known someone, the sense of destinies being tied. Now those words twin with the Sontag quote that took hold of me, the idea of always ending and, simultaneously, always beginning.

After his death I volunteered to help his family by sorting out the storage unit where most of his belongings were. His publisher had arranged for his papers to go to their archive at a university and I wanted to be confident that all the relevant scraps of his work were gathered. I know that when people die, or when families are in crisis, it is hard to take the necessary care needed to spot papers of importance, and I was scared things might be discarded. Over a series of nights, I drove to Catford and pulled out box after box to find his books from his personal poetry library and put them aside – the quiz and trivia books would go to charity. I also looked through tens of boxes of paperwork, intent on rescuing poem drafts, letters and other ephemera of archival importance. I had an urgent sense of mission. But I was also perhaps searching within those papers for anything to indicate my own position in his life, anything to suggest my significance. I was covered in grime, sore from constantly washing and drying my hands. Lifting, tearing, taping, carrying and discarding boxes. This was me trying to get on with things. After a few days off, I returned to work. I remember consulting the absence policy, noting how meagre the allowance is for grief, noticing the definitions of which griefs were worth more leave than others. Friendship was not listed. How could five days be sufficient for any grief? I felt the inadequacy of language and relationship definitions, what we had just not fitting.

I found his school exercise books, full of pencil drawings and his earliest poems, including one called 'Minnie', also the name of one of my cats, that begins 'Minnie can't make up her mind. / Minnie can't make her mind up!' I loved the coincidence and how it made me feel in conversation with Roddy again. I found love letters from past relationships. A metal pencil case belonging to an ex-girlfriend, her name painted on the inside in nail varnish. A tin containing an ancient condom, a lollipop fused to the base, a battery, a passport photo. I found press cuttings and flyers from readings. Pile upon pile of unopened bank statements and bills. A birthday card from his mum that he never opened, which had £25 cash inside. His youth – the time before I knew him – suggested itself to me in these material traces, that familiar blend of hope, sentimentality and denial.

I identified the authors of the love letters and contacted them to ask if they would like me to return them. I felt I needed them to be elsewhere, they were too tempting, as though he were my partner, and I was covertly reading his message history. And in the content of the letters which I'd allowed myself to read, in a skim, as though a skim did not count, I heard the voices of women like me, longing for the love of someone absent, or for the love of someone who was involved with someone else. I was able to return the letters.

I was unbearably touched by this access I had to Roddy's personal effects. I could feel his presence. Even though I found hardly any traces of our relationship in what he left for me to sift through, I am glad I found another way to know him, that the ability to deepen my understanding of him did not cease in his absence. In an essay for the *New Yorker*, Ann Patchett wrote of sorting through and giving away possessions she'd accumulated. Wondering what to do about a small bag of her grandmother's broken, tangled costume jewellery, she said, 'In the end, I decided to let it go, because who in the world would understand its meaning once I was gone?' I admired her for that, but I hope I understood the meaning of Roddy's things, the cuttings and flyers he kept, the receipts, and the lollipop, elastic bands and batteries. And when I die, I hope someone will understand the meanings of mine too.

*

When I love a song, there is almost always a moment that sounds like how I imagine truth to sound, were truth something you could only experience through sound. It's the moment in the song that touches the bruise you didn't know you had, the aching, denied part of you. You are found out by it. In 'River', this point comes when Joni lowers her voice, her register, and sings almost as speech: 'Oh, I wish I had a river'. It is where the wish she has becomes more plaintive, where she is at her most vulnerable. I sometimes wish I could have loved Roddy romantically. I speculate on what that would have looked like. The sex. The meals out. The imbalance of domestic labour. The arguments. I'm certain there would have been arguments. There's still a deluded part of me that believes he'd still be alive if I had. His only religion was romantic love. Grief is described as a kind of love, we're told we only have grief because we have loved. My experiences of grief have revealed to me how distinct a complicated love is from an uncomplicated one. When my grandma died, my mum's mum, my grief contained within it a powerful gratitude for all the happiness and security and loving care she'd given me. I miss her so powerfully, but it is a warm kind of pain; it brings with it no sorrows of things unsaid, harms inflicted, ambitions unmet. Roddy is the complicated grief, the unresolved love to live alongside. *I made my baby say goodbye.*

A little while after I'd completed the task of sorting through Roddy's things, my friend Kayo sent me a cassette player as a house-warming gift. I immediately went to the cassettes I'd saved from Roddy's things, hoping to find a mixtape to listen to, a love token he might have been sent by a girlfriend, or that he'd intended to send. There was a tape that he'd written 'Important' on. I thought I'd start with that. I had an instinct I'd hear his voice on it, perhaps him reading a poem. It was his voice, but it was his singing voice, his beautiful singing voice, singing some songs I did not know. It was the kind of thing I used to do on the first little cassette player I owned – a red one I got for Christmas in the late 80s. I cried of course, listening to him. I cried because I missed him and how we would sing together, but I also cried because of what he might have been hoping to capture in that recording, and for whom it was captured. He was a young man then.

SOUL

part of you pours out of me

In 'A Case of You' Joni sings, 'I remember that time you told me, you said, "Love is touching souls." Surely you touched mine.' It is a pivotal moment, the point at which the song's tender message begins to pour out. I notice, if I look at the lyrics on the page, rather than stitched onto the arrangement of the music, I can find the song's sentiment mildly hysterical. I think it's that word, 'soul'. Saying it aloud I cringe, as though someone has described some clothing as 'trendy'. I'm held back, as if denying an attraction that's taken me by surprise. But I sing along with absolute solemnity. The guitar chords, the music's honest unadornment, balances with the rich blood of the lyrical meaning. So many songs are like this; the music, the notes we hang the words on, make us less self-conscious about the emotional depth in the statements they make. Protect us from words in their naked state. I say this as someone who once sang the whole of Jeff Buckley's album *Grace* to a man I brought home with me and didn't feel embarrassed about having done so until years later.

Almost every time I listen to 'A Case of You', I feel sad I've no one to direct the lyric to when I sing along to it. I summon the defences of romantic lovelessness. Prod the ache repeatedly to check it's still there. It is though, eager to undermine my situation, to designate my life incomplete, I open the windows above a windowsill on which I have arranged the precious totems of my life. Let the rain and wind disrupt and ruin what I felt content with. A deliberate trashing. Like the lack of another soul that I can touch makes my own soul smaller, insubstantial. And I so badly want to have a soul.

The desire for romantic love sometimes builds up behind my temples like a bad weather front. Absence of it from my life is part of how I manifest in the world whether I want to or not. It's pointless to be at war with it, to try to pretend it's not a source of discomfort or confusion or grief. Plenitude of one love doesn't reduce the pain or longing for a type of love you want but don't have. Though I sometimes try to sell myself the idea that it does. Tell myself that the platonic love I have never lacked makes up for, or transcends, the lack of romantic love. I don't buy it. But I know that longing for something doesn't mean life can't be good without it. Or that love songs like 'A Case of You' can't belong to me. It makes me think of my friend Richard Scott's poem 'love version of' where the speaker implores his lover Danny to wake up and 'tell me if the word soul still means anything'. When I first read it, I thought only a lover could use the word 'soul' and get away with it. But it can't be right that I need a lover so that I can speak of having a soul. That doesn't do justice to the role platonic love plays in my life, its endless occasions for consideration of the soul. And it does not recognise the way art enables deep connection to the souls of others, even souls you'll never meet. So even though there is no one specific I sing 'A Case of You' to, I ask myself who and what forms part of what pours out of me in these lines. There's Joni of course, but there's so much more.

*

In January 2019 Camellia and I accompanied Roddy to the T. S. Eliot Prize readings at the Royal Festival Hall, supporting him backstage before the event. In his dressing room I ironed his trousers for him, while Camellia helped him to prepare. He seemed so weak, but on stage, when he gave his reading, he was utterly in control and stood in the applause of his success. I felt so proud of him, not just for the recognition of the short-listing, but for the pleasure he took in it. Afterwards, we took a taxi together to Roddy's care home to drop him off, and then went back to my flat, which Camellia and I had once shared. There we got spectacularly drunk and together tried to come to terms with Roddy's inevitable death. We played each other the songs we had been listening to around that time, ones now forever sewn into the Roddy years. Then we turned backwards towards the songs we had listened to before we had known each other. Songs that did not narrate the complicated grief of our relationships with Roddy. We returned to the threshold of young adulthood. I touched the electric anticipation of Camellia's young soul, and she touched mine.

The next day, hungover and tired, we dressed up again to join Roddy at the T. S. Eliot prize-giving ceremony, along with Roddy's brother Eric. We felt it was unlikely Roddy would win, but we knew he felt hopeful he would, his spectacular faith in his own writing intact. Winning might save him. When Ocean Vuong was announced as the winner and the room exploded with joyful congratulations, including my own, Camellia and I felt Roddy's soul, how quickly it withdrew from the surface of him. Within moments he seemed to have retreated, the internal ticking of his spirit diminished. A year later Roddy was dead. But his soul – I still feel it. When I read his poems, it pours into me. When I read my own poems, and Camellia's, his soul is there too. His soul is present everywhere.

There's an extraordinary long poem I love by the Canadian writer Anne Carson, called 'The Glass Essay'. The speaker of the poem talks of heartbreak, their relationship with their mother, the Brontës. I sometimes read it as the poetic version of the long dark night of the soul. It has a howling, moon-bright clarity, hot and cold transitions of emotion, of thought. It unravels something I try to keep compressed. When the poem's speaker turns to Emily Brontë they worry over the loneliness of Emily's life. No friends, no lovers – 'her raw little soul was caught by no one'. In my own dark nights, this line throbs in my mind like a paper cut. I think I have a soul, even if I'm unsure what it is. Is what I have, what I consider to be my soul, a scrappy raw thing – meat for the birds? When Anne Carson uses the word 'raw', what does she mean? Is an uncooked state an unsolved one, in the way romantic love resolves the puzzle of the self by pairing it with another? Where two souls interact and create a new immaterial, immortal substance, which not only creates something new but alters the originating souls for good? Is romance the only condition for such metamorphosis?

I think of my soul, in its raw state. Bleeding into others, bleeding into my material world, into nothingness. Is this how my soul will leave its trace? Not mixed to a smooth, pleasing consistency with another's through romantic love, one that pours out into something else, making it eternal. Not in the creation or raising of a child, the literal pouring out of part of my self. No, I think, at the mercy of my melodrama, my soul might leave its trace as stains, tackiness across the surface of things, a blot in the soul of another that won't mix properly with their own.

A raw steak is a blue steak. Perhaps my own raw soul is another insinuation of *Blue* into my life, another way I've taken on a blueness, positioned myself in a blue TV-screen light, love lost to me. Cut my soul in half and you'll find blue running through it.

Both cooked and raw things go bad, after a time.

Here I am again in a panic about my raw soul, alienated and ready to take up arms for a failing it's possible that only I am paying attention to. Over and over, it is revealed to me that my idea of my life being partial – because romantic love has not yet rounded it out by pairing me to another – is not because I experience life as partial, but because I tell myself others believe I must. Or I am too ready to believe it when they do. What is that, my vanity speaking? It can seem so. But when that anxiety falls away, when hurt retreats, it becomes clear to me how often my soul meets another's. I've felt it rise to the surface of my body, so that my body has been aglow with it. The occasions that have created that response have been so various – vulnerability, illness, shame, pleasure, community, art. In these states of soulful receptiveness – the giving and receiving of spirit – I'm never a status as drab and suggestive as *being single*.

I think of one occasion, visiting Cork to read at a poetry festival there. My friends Becky, Bryony and Molly came along too. We made a weekend of it. We decided we would visit a museum. The one we went to – Nano Nagle Place – was named after an Irish Catholic woman who founded, in secret, schools for the poor children of Cork, and established her own order of nuns. I'm unsure why we decided to visit this place, but with the vulnerability and disorientation of the hungover, we went there after breakfast. A volunteer greeted us as we approached the museum. She told us Nano Nagle's story. The volunteer, I forget her name, spoke with such passionate admiration for Nano Nagle's work that all of us found ourselves deeply moved, tears forming. A crying quartet. We felt party to a collective emotional experience – the transfer of the volunteer's sincere love for her work, the thoughts of Nano Nagle's mission to help the destitute and dispossessed of her city, the bright stone of the building, the fact we were together, the beautiful sense of our friendships forming, deepening between and across. Threads of it stitching us together back and forth in ever stronger ties. My own emotional response was in part generated by noticing how moved Becky was, how I saw her soul emerging from her, unguarded. All these things mixing, interacting in ways we could not comprehend. It seems ridiculous I ever thought romantic love could be the only true communion of souls. That I did not acknowledge how altered my own soul has been by others and by art. Perhaps great love is the feeling of a collective soul.

Sometimes when two or more of us are together, Becky or Bryony or Molly might suddenly say 'Nano Nagle'. And we all connect again to that feeling.

*

Some people get to consider their soul through religious devotion. It is the part of them that communicates with the divine and keeps them from the devil. For a time in my childhood, the church was a place I encountered the idea of a soul too. My grandparents in Deal were entwined with the work of the church they went to. When visiting, we'd often be taken there when it was closed, and I loved to walk about it while it was empty, to run around the balcony pews and sit at the imposing pipe organ my grandma sometimes played, the wood gleaming caramel in the brittle coastal light. But my soul wasn't moved by the arguments of the sermons: souls were for saving, souls were under surveillance. I'd lie in bed trying to catch God in the act of watching me, trying to drive down my thoughts to a depth God could not travel to. The church in Chatham, where we went to later, had a reward system for kids to encourage them to recite the books of the Bible, a set of coloured pencils with the books of the Bible stencilled on them in gold lettering. I stole a set. That church frightened me.

At that age, music was the thing that made me feel as though I was connected to something larger than myself, perhaps the closest thing to my idea of the divine. I devoted myself to listening, but with my bedroom above the room my dad's piano was in, hearing what he was able to do with the piano, seeing how it calmed him, I also became devoted to the idea of playing.

My dad, delighted I'd taken an interest in his instrument, paid for some piano lessons, which must have been difficult for my parents to afford. I wilfully resisted being taught. This wasn't a rejection of or lack of appreciation for the help I was offered, it was more like my desires couldn't latch on to a formal arrangement. I didn't practise the exercises I was given and made up excuses like 'my dad accidentally took my sheet music to work so I've not been able to'. Instead, I taught myself. I had to write the letters of the notes under the staff notation and because I found rhythm and tempo hard to read, I taught myself that by ear. Painfully, I worked my way through all the piano-led songs I loved and found the sheet music for: Tori Amos's 'Silent All These Years', the Righteous Brothers' 'Unchained Melody', which had a renaissance in the film *Ghost*, the piece River Phoenix plays in *Running on Empty*, the Laura Palmer theme from *Twin Peaks*, 'Rainy Days and Mondays' by the Carpenters and, through a herculean effort, Beethoven's 'Moonlight' Sonata. I wanted to learn how to play Joni's songs too, but I couldn't find the sheet music for them in any local shops. Each song I learned, I learned over many hours, days and weeks. I think now it was one of the most obstinate things I've ever done. It was a practice of love, a soul-deep need. I didn't care how much I was seen to labour over it, make mistakes, show my ardency. My friend Nic and I wrote music together (me on the piano, she on the clarinet), dedicated songs to her dead dog Candy, wrote dreadful chorus-line numbers for the school play. I felt creatively unstoppable. I slipped through time with the piano, fell into the river flow of a greater power. It poured through me.

But in my later teens the piano became obsolete. I had no time for it. I was even a little embarrassed about how earnestly I'd pursued it – trying for anything suddenly felt cringey. As embarrassing as the word 'soul'. I just wanted to dress up in my copycat Gucci velvet hipster flares and vintage platform shoes, paint my eyes with iridescent silver and thick winged liner – get drunk, kiss boys. Music was still vitally important, but I didn't feel the urge to create it myself. Instead, I made mixtapes, carefully arranging suites of songs to propel me through my days and to express desire to another. And then before I knew it, I left home – rushing into my life, ecstatic with the possibilities of disorder – and lived without a piano for the first time. It seemed as though the me who had laboured over my relationship with the piano – something I'd considered essential to my soul's peace – was a vapour. In the years that followed, whenever I encountered a piano, I felt coy. And when I tried to play, only the first few bars of everything I'd taught myself remained in my fingers' memory. I felt a painful loss, as though I'd left a part of myself behind, leaving my soul vulnerable.

Some years ago, a friend emailed to ask for contributions for their partner's fortieth birthday present: a piano. At that time owning a piano seemed to me one of the most adult things you could do – it suggested a home in which a piano could be housed and a domestic situation that would make the playing of a piano an activity that would not require careful negotiation with others living in that space. I contributed to the piano gift fund and tried to tamp down my envy for both the thoughtful partner and the piano. Both felt mythically out of reach.

Then last year, when I was watching TV and moping with some red wine, my friend Ruth sent a voice note to our group chat. It was a recording of Ruth playing the opening bars of 'Blue' by Joni Mitchell on the piano. I don't think I'd known that Ruth had a piano at that point, or at least I'd not paid proper attention to the news that she was learning to play piano in the chat. Hearing it made me cry. The sort of crying that takes you by surprise; fierce emotion had barged in. It sounded beautiful, her playing, the tone of the piano, the song I know and love so well. But I cried not because it was beautiful. I cried because I was deeply, shamefully jealous. The sudden feeling I'd had about wanting a child a few years back was almost paralleled by this desire I felt for a piano. How bodily my yearning for it felt, so that I wanted to howl with the lack of it, how acutely I wanted what she had, felt entitled to it somehow. I've felt so much wanting in my life, but my wants have usually been channelled into material things, with all my desire for love misdirected onto objects. The piano was different. This object desire was also about a relationship I might have, the piano being less material object, more companion, collaborator. A part of my soul I'd abandoned. Despite my envy, the ugliness of it, I felt grateful that I'd identified this need. I finally owned up to what I wanted.

After that night I found myself sitting down at my dining table and stretching out my fingers as though I were laying them on the keys of a piano. Sometimes, when I sat down to write on my laptop, I had a similar sensation: typing as a kind of play, the urge to connect a feeling to an action. I vocalised this intense desire I felt for a piano and to my astonishment my friend Katia sent me a text asking if she could buy me one. I was primed to say, *oh I couldn't possibly let you do that*, but my desire overpowered me. I said yes. She found and paid for a beautiful honey-coloured piano from eBay.

When I called Katia to say thank you, she told me she'd been thinking about how when you're single you don't usually get the huge, special presents that people in relationships sometimes give each other, that they labour over and save up for. She wanted me to have that experience and grant herself the pleasure of giving. A grand, loving gesture was made, and my job was to accept that gift without feeling unworthy of it. I felt so touched. If I learned her songs, my hands would follow the same patterns as Joni's did on her piano. Even if my life hasn't involved the type of big romantic love that *Blue* helped form my vision of, in playing those songs myself, there's some other love taking shape. An incorporation of Joni's music into my own. A possible connection of our souls that can then be shared with others. A thought crosses my mind, a future where I am spoken of in the past tense, *I remember Amy played that on the piano*. I don't need to be good at it, to play it beautifully, just as I don't need to be beautiful. Trying is beautiful. Now that I am learning to play *Blue* on my piano, not just in my interior world, I can give *Blue* to others. People can inherit it from me.

Even though I don't believe in a god, I still feel I am in touch with something beyond myself. Sometimes it's an occurrence timed with such ingenuity it feels cosmic. Like the gift of the piano. Other times, it's a sense of profound connection. One morning my cat settled on the pillow just above my head. It's always my desire for her to do this, but most often she does not; she lies between my legs, or on my hip, and after some minutes I feel the need to move, and she slopes away. But that particular morning she settled and inched her face forward until her cheek rested on my own. It felt like a connection beyond offering her the soft warmth of my body, a cosy place for her to nap. It felt like she was giving herself to me for my comfort alone, letting me lean on her. I felt the friendship of a cat and it touched me. Even though I could easily rationalise the comfort out of it, I let it be taken as I needed to in that moment. My soul needs signs and symbols, not logic.

Perhaps that's why art in all its forms can feel like the purest expression of one soul to another. A means of transcending the boundaried self. It turns out Joni's *Blue* is the case of wine I can drink and still remain standing. Her *Blue* pours out of me, not in a way she might recognise or even find at all touching, but it's there, nevertheless. The soul forever pouring from one to another, making something new through art.

When I was on that trip to LA I went to see an exhibition by the late American artist Ree Morton. I'd been scanning about for something to do and found a listing for it online. The photographs of the show made me think of my friend Anthea's artwork, and I had a sense that in going to see it, I could connect with Anthea, as if temporarily catching a current in which she also swam. I was feeling lonely and wanted something my soul could feel accompanied by. I went early, as soon as the gallery opened, because I prefer to encounter art alone, to be free to move around exhibits at my own pace.

It was in this emotional state that I encountered the work, my want-to-be-alone desire trembling against my need-for-connection desire. I loved everything I saw: her early tentative drawings, embroidered flags, paintings, a sculpture of a see-saw. The pieces that moved me the most were her bright wall-hung sculptures – most featuring text – created using celastic, a fabric that you can mould and then set using a solvent. It has a strange look about it, almost like papier mâché but both waxier and more plastic. It has a quality of warping, giving way and being caught between two forms. I interpreted these pieces as emblems, heraldic crests for women.

One of these, *Don't Worry, I'll Only Read You the Good Parts* (1975), startled me because I began to cry in front of it. The words of the title are painted in black onto a pale butter-yellow panel. Slightly grubby, it drapes and swags at the edges like a magnificent Grecian robe, but also like dirty laundry dropped on the floor for someone else to pick up. It has a yellow flower pinned to the top left of the panel – the shape of a daisy a child might draw. The piece felt like a tribute to the service of others, a tender promise that the 'you' addressed would be spared painful realities the speaker would bear the burden of themselves. It suggested to me an intimate knowledge of the person being addressed, that the speaker could easily separate the good from the bad bits of a story as the 'you' might have experienced them. It was the promise of someone who knew what your soul might need in the moment. I thought of all the times a friend would say to me, 'Don't worry Ames,' or send a text to me, 'dw bb,' adding, 'I love you.' The times that my vulnerable soul was seen and heard and soothed by another. Even if I am uncertain what a soul is, I know a soul is not wholly good, or bad. Perhaps the willingness to share all that the soul contains is what makes soulful connections feel so elusive, not everyone is able to.

When Becky and I were becoming close friends, I insisted I tell her what I perceived as the worst thing I'd ever done, alongside what I felt had been the worst thing done to me. I wanted her to know the edges of my behaviour and experience. Things that had shaped me, shamed me. I needed to know if she could still accept and love me, knowing these things. It was an essentially selfish act on my part. A releasing. But to know someone is to know their bitterness and their sweetness. I don't think you have to love those parts equally. I didn't need her to tell me the thing I'd done was good, I just needed to know whether she saw my humanity within it. My maternal grandma had asked more than once to read my first poetry book and I didn't share it with her. I was afraid she'd see me more clearly and love me less. When she died, I regretted my unwillingness. With Becky, I didn't want to hide parts of myself. I didn't need her to forgive me, I needed to work on forgiving myself, and knew she could help with that.

I thought of this when Roddy was in hospital, his brain fighting toxins that made him say bewildering things. One recurring confession he made was that he'd killed someone. He'd say this to many of us, his brother even sharing that once Roddy had provided so much detail, he felt concerned. Roddy had noticed this and said, 'Don't worry, I've never killed a child or a dog.' He had a vivid, wild look in his eyes when he said these things, as though he was aflame with the thoughts. It did not become a serious part of the conversation that Camellia and I had after our visits to Roddy, often what he told us was such a jumble of outlandish things. Things like he'd won a competition to meet the Beatles or that in the 1600s men had to competitively eat cauliflower and then were charged to use the toilet on a pricing scale determined by the weight of their shit. The number of things I've googled to check if there was a grain of truth in them, including whether the French poet Verlaine had an obsession with potatoes, reviewing a potato dish at a fancy restaurant each month. But more than once Camellia and I asked each other, what if he had killed someone, what then? Would we have been able to undertake the mental feat of making it OK, our love for him remaining intact, in spite of all the bad parts of him we were now aware of? Was this Roddy's illness speaking or was this Roddy seeking redemption? Roddy, terrified of violence, a person who would flinch at seeing someone fall over, who would get weepy looking at an old person because human frailty moved him so much. I think I can be confident Roddy had no bodies buried. But I accepted that I might learn things about him that did not correspond to my relationship with him, my version of his soul, and I would have to find a way of calibrating those in my mind with love. And in a similar way, I am learning and admitting to all the things about myself that I find objectionable. So that I can find ways to reconcile myself with them, act to be better. The art of Roddy's poems is a trail of breadcrumbs I can follow to be close to his soul and all its raucous contradictions. All the poems, all the songs, all the artworks that I've felt adhere to my own soul, perhaps they are the 'you' object I have in mind when I sing 'A Case of You'. The way in which my own soul reaches a fluency. It's a love song where the love's already gone but its traces prevail, have been metabolised into art.

Sometimes my soul feels very peaceful, happy to be contained. Other times it has the urge to send envoys into the world, and I find myself sending unguarded passionate messages, voice notes and even recordings of me singing to my friends. It makes me think of the bit in the song where Joni breaks into the Canadian national anthem. I find the whole song moving, but this particular part, her 'o Canada', sounds like a moment where she forgets the audience and performs in the way you might in a private scene with a lover, family member or friend. No one wants to be a lonely soul, only filled up with yourself and the abstractions of the soul in art. Like a squid stuffed with its own tentacles. A lonely painter, living in a box of paints. But, it occurs to me, needing to identify what or who the 'you' is when I sing Joni's song is another example of my ego troubling with a convention I don't really believe in. My 'you' could be liquid, flowing from one thing to another. It could contain many people and things, be so vast as to be God-sized, an oceanic you. Or it could be small and exact like a square of pure pigment, with a startling itselfness, which once it goes beyond me can transform all it touches.

Six months after Roddy died my grandad died. He was 101 years old. A month before his death, on a family group call, he paused our chit-chat, our talking over one another, to say that he was going to lie down – he felt 'out of puff'. But before he did that, and while he still could, he wanted to say something. 'Thank you for being in my life' was what he said. There was no mistaking his goodbye. I felt something in me liquify. Perhaps it was my sense of my grandad as someone who could never die; I had known him all my life, he and my grandmother were structures I could grow up like ivy scaling the back wall of their house. I was stunned with gratitude for his grace, for his soul's care in saying things that needed to be said – to console him and all of us. I realised I'd forced that so much with Roddy, placed too much significance on a moment where our souls would touch each other and provide mutual solace. Roddy could never have told me what I meant to him, he was too heartbroken and angry that he was losing his life. Roddy also could not bear to hear what he meant to me. But held within the frame of a poem I wrote for him, he could accept it. Could cherish it. I'm glad I was able to give him that.

When the piano Katia bought me arrived, I found a second-hand copy of a Joni Mitchell songbook featuring all the music from *Ladies of the Canyon*, *Blue* and *For the Roses*. I promised myself I would learn the songs one by one, just as I had taught myself to play decades earlier. I'd realised that it wasn't just that my friend Ruth's voice memo had revealed my acute longing for a piano, it had revealed my longing to be able to play Joni's songs myself. What I'd envied was that Ruth could play Joni and I couldn't. I wanted to make *Blue*'s songs my own until I could eventually play by instinct, accompany myself. By the time my birthday came around I could play 'Blue' just about, tentative and unrhythmic, but the song unmistakeable all the same. Very drunk and happy, I played it for my friends – badly. A new quality was present in my life, one that I had hoped for as a child, that one day I would have my own piano, in my own home, and we (I didn't know then who the 'we' would be) would gather around it. Here we were. I was consoled.

DREAMERS

all good dreamers pass this way

Love is transformative, but it doesn't make sense to wait for romantic love to do the work of happiness for you.

In the decade following my parents' divorce, my mum was so sad, so lonely and wretched, I would sometimes not answer her phone calls. I was a coward who couldn't bear how her pain made me feel. She couldn't be a mother as society would expect her to be, as I unfairly expected her to be. Couldn't mask her sadness, demote her own emotional needs for the benefit of her children, and I resented her for it. I was frightened her gloom was something that could absorb me into it, trap me in a miserable amber I might never escape from. I am still ashamed I didn't try harder to soothe her pain, that I took her pain personally, as though it were my burden, not hers.

On a holiday with my sister Rebecca and younger brother Dan, we told her she had to get help. Her sighs had come to feel monumental. When she returned home, she saw a doctor and began to take medication. The lightening effect for her was almost instant. She joined a choir after years of speculating about whether a choir would be something she'd enjoy. She sang her heart out. And then one day Dan borrowed her car and had a minor accident, and her car was out of service, and a man at the choir offered to give her a lift. And then one night he cooked her a meal. And very soon, he loved her. Seeing my mum with someone who loved her, who not only loved her but admired her, found her beautiful, found her interesting, clever, and who found in her someone he wanted to orientate all his plans around, made me so happy. I felt relieved too; I'd been let off the hook, and her happiness once again was snagged onto another.

But it also frightened me that it seemed romantic love is what it took for her to step into herself again, gain access to all her emotional range. Certainly, antidepressants helped too, but it was love that brought about the biggest changes. Yet romantic love cannot be the only thing.

This past winter, spending Christmas alone because my family all caught Covid, I watched *Get Back*, a three-part, eight-hour documentary about the making of the Beatles' live album *Let It Be*. In the second episode, John Lennon asks Ringo Starr to hit his cymbal as a cue, to give him 'the courage to come screaming in'. I felt moved by this, John's soul needing the encouragement of his friend and collaborator to make his entrance, to not only enter but to enter the song with terrific power. So many things have the power to make us the version of ourselves we long for. To step beyond what we thought we were.

One time, I visited Anthea – the friend who I felt connected to via Ree Morton's exhibition – in her studio. On a table was a collection of lichen, arranged in a shallow dish. It smelled like a woollen jumper someone had put on top of their wet swimming costume after leaving the sea. It smelled like a crotch in the sunshine, the earth under a pile of leaves. I fell in love with the lichen. The next time Anthea and I saw each other, she gave me a box of it – some formed on small branches, some that looked like dried sea creatures taken from a beach. Lichen is a form created through the partnership of algae and fungi – two organisms functioning as a single unit. Together they create something new, but they have integrity in their former state. They were not less before, or more now. It would be pointless to look at fungi and wish it were lichen, when fungi has so much of interest and beauty in it. Like wishing blue were green.

I now come to see blue wherever green is present, and green in the presence of blue. *No end and no beginning*. It wasn't just that visual experience I had in LA, where the partnership of the two colours was abundant in the natural world, it was Joni's songs that did that too. In 'Little Green', her child's eyes – so named that winter will not fade her – 'are blue'. In 'River', when California is unwilling to give her a real winter, its emphatic greenness intensifies her heartache. Green and blue have become notes in a chord that plays in my mind whenever I think of what love means to me. The constancy of love interests me less than the ways in which our experience and ideas of love can alter. Love is a living thing, with green edges of new growth, even the love you feel for the dead.

As much as Joni sought to slip out of the place she was in, the state she was in, she longed for an anchor. She sought the warm chords of her home. A dark café she could cocoon herself in. The more I've listened to what she says in *Blue*'s songs, the more comforted I am about my own messy desires. The way I've hated some and loved some. My need for retreat and escape, the way I weave back and forth between apparently contradictory or paralleled feelings, creating a cocoon of indecision.

I hear this ambivalence all throughout *Blue*. In one track she listens to a song on her headphones that goes 'goodbye baby, baby goodbye', then sings her own song about making her 'baby say goodbye'. Her lover is mean, but she likes him. She sings the most beautiful love song for a lost love, but commemorates that love within it, makes it feel eternal, a love that has no end and no beginning. She wants to skate away, but she doesn't want to be the figure skater wife, placated by a dishwasher, whose husband sits by the light of a TV each night. She doesn't know what she's looking for, but she is able to list everything she wants. *Blue* is a lens through which she sees so many things, sees so many shades of life – her home, a lover's name, a child's eyes, sadness, travel, grief, sex, desire, renewal. I want to say to her, *I hear you, Joni.*

I know there's a chance someone will read my story and think, *twenty-two years alone, that's nothing! Wait until it's thirty, wait until it's forty!* Their head shaking at my naivety, the self-importance in my sadness. I understand that impulse. If we don't get what we are supposed to want and be fulfilled by, can we at least feel special in our lack? I ask myself now whether my romantic lovelessness has become so enormous as to be impressive, noble, a string to my bow? Am I scared to give that up? Have I become too committed to this way of life, my own little pilgrim? It strikes me how easy it is to present myself as a sad, self-deprecating little calamity, and this has been a way to remain hidden from myself. While it's true that I've never wanted to be defined by my relationship to a man, to a romantic partner, I realise I don't want to be defined by the lack of one either. I thought perhaps I had to choose. And I thought perhaps I had to hide my hurt. Pretending not to hurt is worse than pretending to be happy. You can't hold in hurt and expect it not to grow.

It's awkward when you've maintained a position for so long. Like when you double-down in an argument and don't know how to give yourself a way out. It seems it costs a lot to change your mind. Or like how frightening it can be to say you are sorry – there's a risk you won't be forgiven. Or admitting the thing you felt was a thing you felt at a particular moment, and it might be possible to feel differently. Watching that feeling skate by you and away. I understand the stakes. I don't want to claim lovelessness as a way of life, assign myself to a category of person, flinching each time I have to tick a box to indicate my status. I want romantic love. Its absence creates a real pain, but I've come to understand some of that pain is generated by an assumption that people are watching my aloneness, people are judging it, pitying it. I told myself life was withholding from me all the things I connected to romantic love. But it wasn't. That was a lie I hoped might soothe me by making everything I wanted an impossible dream, and with that I might find acceptance for my lot.

*

Last summer I was at a party. There was strange weather. Bleats of sunshine, feeble rain, the irregular chill of cloud cover. It was in one of the reprieves where pandemic lockdown restrictions were lifted. Though desperate and giddy for novelty in human contact, no one knew how to socialise. We'd been cut loose from our anchors. In the mildness of the atmosphere, for a time we swayed gently on our spots. The hours flicked by. Without noticing, we found ourselves adrift.

Midway through, a younger woman I don't know very well talked to me for a while. We got to talking about being single. She identified with me – told me she lived without romantic love and couldn't understand why. She cried a little. I commiserated. But then a more dismissive attitude rose in me, the aversion to seeing yourself reflected in another person. I told her she was young and not to worry. She wasn't like me at all. I was impatient for her to see she was OK really, and of course love would come along – she was young! She was beautiful!

But ten years ago, I was her. I was young. And here I am trudging into my mid-forties. Nothing has changed. I lied to her thinking it would soothe her in her moment of distress. And I know I failed her. She probably felt invalidated by this *one person* who she'd thought would know what it was like to be her. The experience of living at the edge of how other people organised and planned their lives. Felt denied the one thing that was supposed to make us whole, give us purpose. The thing that performs the mysterious act of connecting our intimate, sexual, domestic, familial, social, spiritual and cultural lives: romantic love.

It's only recently I realised I did this. The memory of it emerging as I tried to get to sleep, becoming a sticky thought that lasted beyond the night. I'd let her down when I could have offered my genuine solidarity. When I had been her age, I got drunk and shared my pains with near strangers. I felt fobbed off, infuriated and embarrassed when they responded with platitudes. Then the next day I'd wake early with anxious shame, sending messages of apology for my tears, my oversharing, ready for people to read when they got up. I wanted to get to them quickly, make sure they knew I knew my failings. I knew I was too much.

I wish I could have said to the young woman, you might not get the romantic love you so badly want, but you'll be OK.

You'll live alongside it, and though there will be bad days when it really makes its presence felt, there'll be good days, lots of them. But I couldn't. I didn't believe it. I had no hopeful offerings to make, I did not feel OK. I wanted to draw the conversation to a close so I could talk trash with my friends. Drink some more. Get some clandestine hugs – the absence of physical touch for so long had made me feel peculiar, as though I needed someone to trace the edges of my body to confirm I was in the world. I excused myself from the conversation with the younger woman and went into the kitchen to find more wine. My friend offered me a tequila shot instead. I filled my wine glass and took the shot too. Then another. I let myself go into the pull of a current.

Later on, as if to punish me for my unwillingness to speak honestly to this younger woman, I lay down on my friend's sofa, irredeemably drunk. 'I am never going to be loved,' I wailed, tears sliding from one eye, mixing into the tears from the other and splatting on the wooden floor. Absolutely inconsolable. I can't promise that will be the last time.

After the party I had to find within my shame at so publicly giving myself away a means by which I could face my feelings. I decided I could not continue to live like this, with all my emotional mess around me, finding endless reasons not to say what I wanted to say.

I need to cross a threshold – from the place I am in now, where I can still feel confused, ashamed, embarrassed, angry even, that romantic love is not part of my life, to a place where I care less about what other people might think about me and don't punish myself when I do care, judge myself less for always wanting more. I have to own that romantic love is a present desire, not consigned to some fantasy me.

I grew up expecting romantic love, assuming its glorious, wild presence would be a natural part of life's journey. I wanted it. When it didn't come, or at least wasn't reciprocated, I was told it was because I was wanting it a little too much, and that it would happen when I least expected it. You can't trick yourself out of expecting something. But I got something I wasn't expecting. I loved Roddy and was transformed by that love. He once said I was like 'a strange moment in a clearing'. Perhaps he was transformed by me too.

I still hope there is romantic love to come – I cannot give up hoping for it, but I don't want to become unravelled by jealousy for everything that is not. I don't want to pay attention to the epiphanic declarations of people with different experiences to me and use them as evidence that my life's experience can never be equal to theirs. I must find my way to a life that is good as it is. Though it's true that I have for some years tried to protect myself from romantic love's worst affects, this hasn't reduced my capacity for the emotional intensity romantic love can generate. I've not experienced a dormancy of feeling. But I did need to look closely at my life and reach for the love in it. There is almost too much for me to bear. Certainly too much for me to have noticed properly before. That's the risk of abundance. It can be easy to find it lacking. A birthday party where you're sore someone didn't come rather than delighting in all who did. A canyon of want that is impossible to fill.

It wasn't until recently that I paid attention to a line in *Blue*'s first song that goes, 'I love you when I forget about me.' In the last few years, I've come to realise that in the romantic loving I've done, I've often obliterated my sense of self: I've not located my needs, let alone asked for them to be met. I've just doggedly pursued a kind of abstract reciprocation – have I been noticed or have I not? – and because I've not paid enough attention to what I want, the vast contrast between what I want and what I've received hasn't been as visible to me. Romantic love transformed me but not in the way I'd dreamed it would. It made me forget myself, not to my self's flourishing advantage – connected, inspired, courageous – but to my detriment. My resilience, self-image and facility for care scrawny with neglect.

When I started to write this book, I was worried my idea of being in love – how *Blue* had formed it – might be based on fiction, a naive acceptance of storytelling as truth. I hoped that I could find within my own experience ways in which my love for *Blue* and the ideas it gave about love were present despite romantic love's absence; evidence that life doesn't have to be a quest to find a romantic someone to be a good, full life. I think I've found that. But as I've been writing, I've also realised I want to find a way to have romantic love in my life without forgetting myself and all I can generate alone.

When I have thrown coins into fountains and wells, it has been with a private wish for love. When I've blown the candles out on my birthday cakes. When I have drawn a card from the tarot, it has been in the hope for guidance about how to find love. When on one summer solstice I wrote something I wanted to manifest on a piece of paper and added it to the communal fire, that thing was romantic love. If I catch a shooting star, scatter the seeds of a dandelion clock with my breath, see a double fucking rainbow. None have yet been granted. I still wish.

In 'All I Want' Joni sings, 'All I really, really want our love to do, is to bring out the best in me and in you too'. If my therapist, rather than asking me to write a list of what I wanted in a romantic partner, had asked me to write a list of what I want from my life now, what would bring out the best in me, I feel I could attempt to write that list. And through it dream myself into a new beginning and be brave enough to ask for it. These are the wants I would set out for my life:

I want to topple romantic love from its central position, hierarchy being at odds with love. I can want romantic love at the same time as valuing and being fulfilled by what is present in its absence.

My home is perfect as it is. Even if I one day share a home with another human, I want to always remember how marvellous it is to live alone, and I want to retain an open sense of what a family home can be.

I want mothering to be part of my life. To offer and receive loving care and support with friends, family members and my cats. I stretch mothering to hold those things. When I grieve not having a child, I want to remind myself those feelings pass; I want to let myself feel what I feel without attempting to tidy those emotions up into neat resolutions. Though I did not act on my body's temporal utility, I retain my own powers of creation.

I want to be a good friend to myself, do things that tend to me without becoming puritanical, commodified and in debt. I no longer hold myself hostage to self-love.

I want to embrace and create intimacy. In an interview Joni once said that she thought *Blue* had helped people to 'face their *own* intimacy'. This has been true for me.

I want to keep travelling, and to accept myself wherever I am. I let myself try and fail in the pursuit of pleasure.

The question we can so often ask ourselves in the debris of romantic failure is *what did I do wrong? What is wrong with me?* A friend might encourage you to ask instead *what was wrong in that relationship for me?* So, though I want to delight in sex and pursue romance, I want to refuse sex and romance that erupts into self-loathing. Whatever those relationships might look like, however much I desire them, if that is happening, they are not right for me.

I recognise the loves that I have, and I cherish them all, without letting the fear of loss take love's possibility away from me.

I let my soul roam freely to seek the consolation and collaborative potential of art, friendship and vulnerability. This is how I get to be me.

I deserve to dream a good dream of the future. I've stopped waiting for it to begin.

These are my own chords of inquiry. The dream songs I've written to *Blue*'s arrangements.

*

I have never tired of *Blue*. Perhaps the reason I can listen to it with as much emotional candour as that first time back in my teenage bedroom with the lava lamp doing its mysterious work is because I've no object to attach to the songs. That might be something to be grateful for – in the past I've had to give up whole musical genres because they were too closely aligned with a source of romantic pain.

At times when I've been writing, I've felt worried that in paying so much attention to something I've loved, something that's given me solace, been a formative event, I'd destroy it. I keep listening to *Blue*, as though to check it is still mine, still moves me as it always has. I can't bear to love *Blue* and lose it. Break it through overuse. But this isn't what I've found. *Blue*'s still intact, my feelings are still intact. My love of *Blue* can survive interrogation. And I know that when I love *Blue*, and share my love for it, I'm part of something. I've loved it so much my love has bled into the love that others have for it. A collective love.

Blue is something I will always be able to step into, reflective like a deep pool of still water, edgeless as the night sky. My notions of love have been encoded in *Blue* for decades, and stepping into it now, I understand those notions are broader than romantic love; I found all other loves in *Blue* as well.

On *Blue*'s last song, 'The Last Time I Saw Richard', Joni's voice moves with such agility between syllables and notes, she's like a mountain goat that scrambles up and down a rock face while you stand at the bottom, tense with disbelief and hope. I'm reminded of Joni's thoughts on *Blue*, 'there's hardly a dishonest note in the vocals'. I'd go further – by the time we reach the end of the album, Joni seems sonically fearless.

Joni rebukes the Richard of the title for 'romanticising pain'. This is the trap I didn't know I'd fallen into. On her album *Ladies of the Canyon* – the one that came before *Blue* – there is a song called 'Willy', which feels to me like the gateway to *Blue*'s sensibilities. In that song she sings about how if you let fear get in the way of loving, you'll always lose out. I would apply that logic to the men I have desired. They were just too scared to feel for me and I was the brave woman who put her heart in harm's way. What I've realised is that I'm also Richard from Joni's song, who needs Joni to say 'love can be so sweet', and to ask me 'when you gonna get yourself back on your feet?'

I'm no longer going to identify myself with failure, allow my big emotions, resentments and desires to burn holes in my self-esteem. I refuse to let what I lack remain the organising principle of my life. I hope to be transformed, not through the neat solution of finding love or persuading myself I don't want it. I hope for more – for plenty – of those other, quieter transformations. The ones that make you feel the world all around you. Like the year Roddy died, when I saw some friends for the first time in months, to celebrate my birthday. Months of dreaming, of existing in the darkness of solitude and grief, came briefly to an end. We sat outside my flat drinking, and a thunderstorm came in. Recognising the romantic potential of a storm, I stood out in the rain and gave myself over to what heavy rain could activate in my body. Rain so heavy it felt like being touched. Later that evening, there were just three of us left. I asked if they wanted to sing *Blue* with me. And we sang.

Acknowledgements

First, to my agent Angelique Tran Van Sang. I feel so lucky to work with you, not just for your patience and tremendous skill as an editor, but for your friendship and hand-holding as I encountered the vulnerabilities of making a book. Few things have made me feel as afraid, but your weather reports, encouragement, and invitations to celebrate have brought me so much comfort and pleasure. I hope we get to do this together again!

To my editor Željka Marošević. You're not only my ideal editor but my ideal reader. It still feels astonishing to me that this happened. Every question and comment you made on the manuscript, and every conversation we had, improved this book. I hope we sing *Blue* together one day. Thanks also to Michal, Cecile, Rowena, Mia, Saba, Hannah, Emma and everyone at Jonathan Cape who worked on the book.

To my wonderful US agent Alison Lewis for making a dream come true. To my brilliant US editor Gina Iaquinta – I'm so grateful you immediately understood the story I wanted to tell and for your shaping of it. Thank you to Zeba Arora and everyone at Liveright.

Some of the material in this book is adapted from essays I wrote for the *Granta* website, the anthology *At The Pond*

(Daunt Books) and the 'This Artwork Changed My Life' column on *Elephant* magazine's website. I'm grateful to the editors who commissioned me: Eleanor Chandler, Sophie Missing and Louise Benson. I doubt that this book would exist if Eleanor had not accepted my pitch to write about 'Joni Mitchell and poets' and conjured out of me an altogether different story. Thank you, Eleanor, I'll never forget our phone call to talk about the first draft of 'A Bleed of Blue.'

I'm grateful to several people who gave me advice about how to get this book into the world including Kishani Widyaratna, Olivia Laing, Katherine Angel and Sarah Perry. I'm also very grateful to Arts Council England for a Developing Your Creative Practice grant that gave me the confidence and freedom to explore moving from poetry to prose. Big thanks to Karen McCarthy Woolf and Sophie Herxheimer for having me stay while I was in California.

Roddy Lumsden called a book's *Acknowledgements* 'the first poem' and would always turn to it first. It's painful that he will never read these ones, but if I can allow myself to imagine he could I would say to him: Roddy, you will always be a landmark of my life. I owe you so much.

I hope anyone who reads this book will come to know Roddy and his wonderful poems a little. I'm also very grateful to Roddy's family, in particular Eric Lumsden.

I can't believe that because I wrote this book, I ended up on the phone to Mary Margaret O'Hara. Thank you, Mary Margaret, for allowing me to quote 'To Cry About', a song that is so important to me.

To my family for giving me the room to speak and loving me for it. Especial thanks to my sister Rebecca for the inheritance of Joni, and to my mum, Sue – I'm so proud of you.

So many friends have offered encouragement, enthusiasm and advice as I wrote this book:

I'm so grateful to my pals Jane Yeh, Richard Scott, Alex MacDonald and Crispin Best for being my lovely gang and enduring more book-related celebrations than some might find reasonable. To Anwen, Laura, Ruth, Tana, Emily and Nischalasri for your enduring loving friendship. To Lorraine for your mischief and care. To Anthea for always inspiring me.

To Amy Blakemore, Sophie Davidson, Rebecca Tamás, Rebecca May Johnson, Lucy Mercer and Eli Goldstone for conversations that made me feel more powerful than is probably advised. To Molly Rosenberg for always being ready to sing Joni with me. To Katia Wengraf for the piano and the spectacular comfort of feeling seen. To Rachel Benson for being the person I always want to be at the party.

To Bryony White for showing me I can be someone who lives 'together' rather than alone. For your intelligence, integrity and ability to make me have so much fun.

To Camellia Stafford for the incredible gift of your friendship, compassion, and support. I cannot do without it.

To Rebecca Perry for saying 'I'm your person' and letting me hold you to it. I'm forever altered by it. I love you so much.